Transform Product Requirements Management and Value Delivery

An Agile Approach to Creating Excellent Digital Products

Table of Contents

CHAPTER 1: BEFORE THE NEW SYSTEM 13

THE AS-IS ANALYSIS 14
AREAS OF CHANGE 15
THE TO-BE SYSTEM..15
SYSTEM PROPOSAL (BUILDING THE BUSINESS CASE FOR THE NEW SYSTEM).............16
SOFTWARE DEVELOPMENT PHASES 18

CHAPTER 2: IDENTIFY AND ELICIT REQUIREMENTS 29

IDENTIFY NEEDS..33
BUILD ORGANIZATIONAL CONTEXT 34
STAKEHOLDERS DISCOVERY 35
REQUIREMENTS ELICITATION..41

CHAPTER 3: PROTOTYPE AS A REQUIREMENT GATHERING TOOL 53

EXECUTING THE SPRINT 54
PROTOTYPING TO REALIZE THE VALUE IN UNCERTAIN CONDITIONS........................57
DISCOVER REQUIREMENTS USING PROTOTYPES...61
STAGES OF REQUIREMENTS DISCOVERY AND USER FEEDBACK CAPTURE..................64

CHAPTER 4: GATHERING, PRIORITIZING, ANALYZING, AND MANAGING
REQUIREMENTS 67

GATHERING REQUIREMENTS 67
PRIORITIZING REQUIREMENTS 75
ANALYZING REQUIREMENTS 80
CREATE SYSTEMS TEST CASES...81
BUILD PRODUCT ROAD MAP 84
THE REQUIREMENTS DOCUMENT 86

CHAPTER 5: PROJECT EXECUTION APPROACH (AGILE APPROACH) 89

EXTREME PROGRAMMING 92

SCRUM 94

LEAN SOFTWARE DEVELOPMENT 97

KANBAN 98

VALUE STREAM MAPPING 99

AGILE AT SCALE 100

CHAPTER 6: FINDING THE BEST MIX FOR THE BEST BUSINESS VALUE 103

POSSIBLE FORMS OF VALUE DELIVERY 103

BUILD THE ROAD MAP TO OPTIMIZE VALUE 106

CHAPTER 7: PROJECT EXECUTION 113

PROJECT JOURNEY 113

PHASE ONE: CHARTERING AND TEAMBUILDING 114

PHASE TWO: DISCOVER USERS' NEEDS (USER STORIES) 115

PHASE THREE: DEVELOP HIGH-LEVEL ARCHITECTURE 117

PHASE FOUR: RELEASE PLANNING 120

PHASE FIVE: DELIVERY, BUILD, LEARN, AND IMPROVE 122

PHASE SIX: UAT AND TRAINING 123

PHASE SEVEN: DEPLOY TO PRODUCTION 125

BONUS CHAPTER: AGILE PHILOSOPHY 127

WHAT IS COMPLEX? 127

TYPES OF COMPLEX SYSTEMS 128

ADDING TIME 131

Table of Figures

Figure 1 IT-TNG framework 10

Figure 2 Ten practices stack 11

Figure 3 Book map... 12

Figure 4 System creation cycle 14

Figure 5 Software development... 19

Figure 6 Activity main ingredients.. 20

Figure 7 Definitions hierarchy 20

Figure 8 Application building blocks.. 21

Figure 9 Project team roles 22

Figure 10 Development life cycle 24

Figure 11 Branching codes 25

Figure 12 Stakeholder diagram 36

Figure 13 Overall process 37

Figure 14 User groups 38

Figure 15 Application audience 41

Figure 16 Workshop structure 44

Figure 17 Story mapping 50

Figure 18 Storyboard.. 51

Figure 19 Uncertainty and scope 54

Figure 20 Design sprint.. 55

Figure 21 Features progress 56

Figure 22 Design sprint and prototype cycle....................................... 56

Figure 23 Prototype and burn-down.. 57

Figure 24 Three levels of prototyping 58

Figure 25 Types of native prototypes.. 60

Figure 26 Incremental, evolutionary, and evolutionary–incremental
prototyping... 61

Figure 27 Requirements clarification using prototypes 63

Figure 28 Prototype testing... 65

Figure 29 Requirements taxonomy 70

Figure 30 Competition analysis 71

Figure 31 Commonality and risk.. 75

Figure 32 Commonality analysis.. 76

Figure 33 The cone of uncertainty 78

Figure 34 Use case diagram... 81

Figure 35 Purpose alignment model 85

Figure 36 Features and road map 86

Figure 37 Spiral 90

Figure 38 Flow pipeline 91

Figure 39 Relation between the spiral and the pipeline 91

Figure 40 Agile project phases 94

Figure 41 Backlog chart example 95

Figure 42 Agile and Waterfall mix 103

Figure 43 Requirements in Agile native 104

Figure 44 Requirements in Waterfall 105

Figure 45 Requirements for Waterfall and Agile delivery 105

Figure 46 Economics of Agile 107

Figure 47 Cost versus value 109

Figure 48 Velocity 110

Figure 49 Value in chunks 110

Figure 50 Throwaway solutions 111

Figure 51 Project types 113

Figure 52 Agile project journey 114

Figure 53 BA schedule 116

Figure 54 Design levels 118

Figure 55 Main design 118

Figure 56 Design with developed features 119

Figure 57 Release planning 120

Figure 58 Release burnup 121

Figure 59 Task board 122

Figure 60 System complexity 131

Figure 61 Time and complexity 132

Figure 62 Sustaining system complexity 132

Tables

Table 1 Negative requirement 52
Table 2 Coding table...71
Table 3 Requirements categories...72
Table 4 Ambiguous words...73
Table 5 Interaction matrix..74
Table 6 Commonality table 76
Table 7 Relationship matrix...77
Table 8 Prioritization calculation...79
Table 9 Product road map..84
Table 10 Kanban 99
Table 11 Team types 115

Preface

After working as a consultant for 19-plus years now—meeting customers daily, attending workshops, and listening to business issues to develop solutions—I wondered why IT transformation often fails to deliver the expected results. It took me a few years to gather enough knowledge across multiple fields to build a big picture. During the journey, I discovered, much to my surprise, that information technology organizations fail in the basics, or even neglect some components, leading to a deficit in the digital transformation. This was when I started drafting the IT transformation guide for the next-generation IT (IT-TNG framework).

The *IT-TNG framework* is focused on practitioners, not on theoretical knowledge. Each guide helps a practitioner achieve a specific function using tested methods and concepts from the industry. I also wanted to empower the readers in their careers by including a bit of business in the books. This is relevant because when a subject matter expert like a developer, business analyst (BA), or administrator understands topics like strategy, decision-making, and value, their management typically notices, which is often advantageous in their careers.

Each book balances theories, practical steps, and management practices. This structure aims to empower whoever reads these books in their current role and provide them with the knowledge to take a more prominent role in the organization.

The IT-TNG framework consists of the following practices:

- Process: Process reengineering
- Digital solution: How to develop a digital solution
- Solution HL design: Align requirements to design
- Services: How to build a service offering to the customer
- Value support: How to support a service in the best possible manner
- Value maintenance: How to control the technical aspects of a service

- Service adjustments: Decision-making and service components adjustment
- Value realization: Promote and discover services
- Innovation: Generate innovative ideas to solve business challenges
- Strategy and effort orchestration: Developing synergies from all practices

Figure 1 *IT-TNG framework*

Each of these modules is independent, and although each represents a layer in IT that should not be neglected when considering digital transformation, two or more practices generate synergy and start driving improvement. A single practice will drive value, but you need at least three practices to drive the digital transformation forward.

The organization might already have a functioning practice representing one aspect of the IT-TNG. In such a case, keep it as is. The idea is to build the missing parts of the 10 core practices regardless of efficiency. And once you create the whole stack, you can go back to optimize these practices.

While writing the IT-TNG, I followed a focused approach with two principles in mind:

- 80/20 rule
- Law of diminishing returns

The 80/20 rule means you don't need many initiatives to achieve the best results. You only need a handful of initiatives to reach a strategic position. The law of diminishing returns means that with every improvement, you gain less, so it's about finding the pressure point and pressing to get the maximum results with the least effort. I also considered the unintended effects of applying these practices. For example, thinking critically about a software design unintendedly challenges the value, reduces change requests, and increases business alignment.

This is what all of these practice guides are about, the minimum possible resource investments that will drive value.

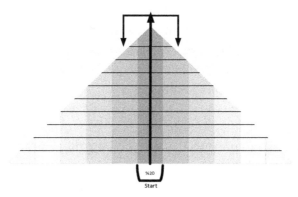

Figure 2 Ten practices stack

The practices have no specific order, but there are 10 levels. Start with the core activities in each layer, and once all ten practices are stacked, you begin expanding each practice layer based on the organization's need. If you try to grow one layer before making the core stack of all 10 layers, you will hit the collective ceiling blocking value realization, regardless of investment. To avoid hitting this and wasting resources, you should build the initial layers first to proceed in a value-adding manner.

How to Get in Touch with Me

You might have a question or need clarification to adapt the ideas discussed in this book to your situation. Please feel free to drop me an email at Ahmed.Hussein@ITTNG.com.

About This Book

This book is about creating a digital product in an agile manner. However, I am not focusing on the technologies used during the project. I am focusing on building the practice to align the business value to the generated value, though this book is independent in explaining the execution part of the project. Additional requirements need to be found or adjusted during the project to populate or clean the backlog.

On the other hand, sometimes you are thrown into the middle of a project, and you are expected to perform as well. This guide can be used in both cases. However, the second case will require you to change course and perform code refactoring more often to incorporate the additional requirements. This methods in this book (step 3 in Figure 3) should be executed within seven days to generate the initial requirements of the first sprint. Investing an additional two weeks in building the initial understanding and the application models with the subject matter expert (SME) (step 2) will save you a great deal of effort during the project and prevent lots of rework.

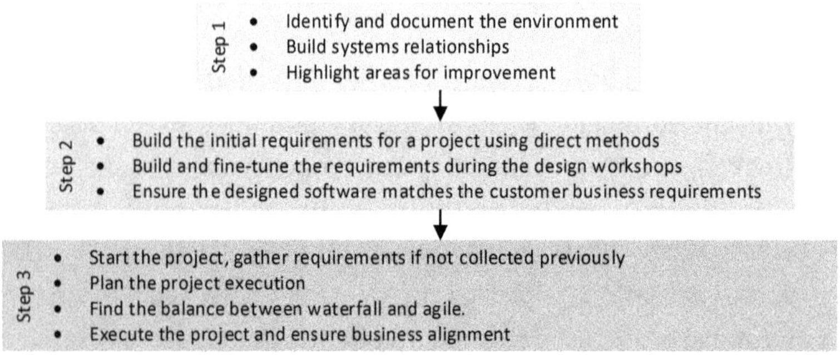

Step 1
- Identify and document the environment
- Build systems relationships
- Highlight areas for improvement

Step 2
- Build the initial requirements for a project using direct methods
- Build and fine-tune the requirements during the design workshops
- Ensure the designed software matches the customer business requirements

Step 3
- Start the project, gather requirements if not collected previously
- Plan the project execution
- Find the balance between waterfall and agile.
- Execute the project and ensure business alignment

Figure 3 Book map

Chapter 1: Before the New System

••••••••••••••••••••••••••••

Typically, a new system is generated from a business requirement, and the solution usually involves one of the two following options:

Prepackaged application. A prepackaged application is used with well-established practices, like finance, HR, and so on. Such a system is used for noncore business systems. And, as mentioned, customization in such an application is still necessary, but it's limited to adjusting the software to meet the organization's needs, like adjusting the business processes and reporting systems such as enterprise resource planning (ERP).

Custom-based application. The focus starts on the business vision and strategy. This application is typically custom-made for the organization to solve a specific problem, and maybe provide a competitive edge.

Knowing which scenario you face will impact the system creation process since some parts might not be required with the prepackaged system. Let's explore how to plan system creation and discern the process flow. Understanding the big picture will help deliver a more agile value to the business. Whether you approach this task from the standpoint of a business system (big picture) or business process (detailed steps), remember that your strategy must produce the expected required value, or potential business will be lost. So, when building a business system, consider the entire process.

System creation involves five steps:

Step 1: The as-is analysis: Determine current actions.

Step 2: Areas of change: Highlight areas that need changes.

Step 3: The to-be system: Review the old system and propose a new system to accommodate the required enhancements.

Step 4: System proposal: Generate a system request or system proposal.

Step 5: Software development

In an existing system, proceed through steps 1 to 5. For a new system, skip step 1.

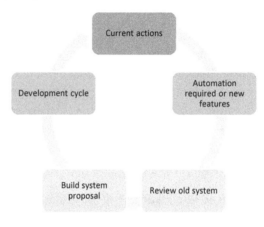

Figure 4 *System creation cycle*

Before starting the cycle, evaluate whether it is worth the investment. A feasibility analysis will enable you to develop the answer.

The as-Is Analysis

The first step is to know the organization's current operational status. The "as-is" analysis must precede calling for any improvements or making any adjustments to the current setup. Any uncalculated move, such as trying to impose a new process or develop a capability that runs counter to the existing operations, can result in project failure.

Start by documenting the existing process and system using multiple diagrams. Documentation is typically the role of the business analyst or the functional consultant if you don't have an analyst in your organization.

The diagrams should help provide clarity on what is needed to move forward. Typically, hundreds of processes exist in any given organization. Upgrading or modifying any components requires understanding who is responsible for each component and identifying the data used. Any decision will require a sufficiently deep knowledge of entities, activities, and data flow. Here is a brief overview of how to create the as-is analysis.

How to Document Current Systems

There is a strong chance that the organization's documentation is outdated. Start by documenting the existing system.

Create an Activity List

An activity list contains simple interviews with the owners overseeing functions. Drill down deep into each interaction.

Consult with the owner if one is available. If not, go to the frequent users and ask how the processes flow with all their variations. It is much like a what-if scenario. When a new branch diverges from an activity, start a new list. Document the narrative, and begin building the activity table. Once the activity table is ready, extract the following:

1. Context diagram
2. Physical data flow diagram (PDFD)
3. Logical data flow diagram (LDFD)
4. Flowchart

Areas of Change

These are the newly discovered requirements, high-level business requirements, or problems that need a solution.

The to-Be System

This step is all about drawing the needed diagrams, the wireframes, and the ERD diagrams—tools that will help plan the to-be system. A traditional application is a combination of:

- Interface (screens to enter or display data)
- Objects/entities or classes
- A method/activity or action (what it will solve)
- A gate to validate the application actions (business rules)
- The overall process flow
- The databases (to store the data)

- The reporting (the data generated and arranged in a particular way to be helpful for the end user)

Each layer is addressed through different diagrams and models. Most diagrams can be used in any layer, although some are designed to bring greater clarity to a designated layer and are not interchangeable. Exploring these diagrams to learn where each can be employed is key to delivering the correct message.

The business analyst (BA) should be able to define the requirements of all layers, their restrictions, and their respective databases. The analyst also must know the requirements of the associated business application. This inquiry will give you important insights and perspectives. Such deep system requirements can be collected only during the design workshops with the subject matter experts and the customer/end user. However, the role of the BA is only to ensure that the requirements match the expectations and are defined in a clear way. This deep understanding will allow the BA/product manager to determine the customer's behavior during the project.

A specialized solution designer takes the to-be transition to the next level and designs a tailor-made solution. As the business analyst, you will interact with several leading solution developers (subject matter experts) to define their requirements and work jointly to refine the requirements during the design workshops. This shared understanding will be the system's foundation and the principle guiding all aspects of the software development process. It might even be codified into guiding principles that will allow the team some decision-making flexibility and ensure faster response time during the project.

System Proposal (Building the Business Case for the New System)

Generate a system request or system proposal. This is the business case of the system. Here are the fixed and most basic guidelines. Others can be added as needed. But in all cases:

Stay on point. Be brief so management can quickly read the business case. Do not exceed a few pages.

The business case will be negotiable. Management may suggest other areas of focus or may wish to cut costs. In those cases, reevaluation of the business case options may be appropriate.

Here are the basics of writing the business case:

Part 1. Executive summary: This is a paragraph explaining the purpose of the business case. Typically, this is written by a businessperson and placed at the beginning of the document, even though it is the final piece to be written.

Part 2. Problem definition (analysis): Outline business issues. Include all issues related to quick wins so management will be eager to resolve and willing to support them.

Part 3. Goals: List the desired outcomes.

Part 4. Solutions: Outline the options to solve each given problem. For each solution, define these factors:

- **Assumptions**: Assume that the project will be able to proceed as intended.
- **Outcomes and benefits**: Outline the benefit of each option.
- **Cost**: Calculate or estimate the cost for each option.
- **Timeline**: Determine how long it will take to implement each option.
- **Risk assessment**: List the risks of deploying each option. Present other options that can produce different levels of costs, risks, and outcomes.

Part 5. Recommendation: Describe the best option and explain why it is recommended.

Part 6. Appendices (optional): In the appendices, add a financial analysis. Though this may be the most challenging part of the business case, it is helpful to demonstrate the prospective outcome with supporting data such as revenue, total cost, break-even point, fixed cost, payback period, net present value, and internal rate of return.

By generating the system proposal, you completed the first part of the new system. Once the system proposal is approved, the project is started. And the starting point is to define the software development process.

Software Development Phases

Usually, software development as a whole goes through four primary phases:

1. Project initiation
2. Requirements and specifications
3. Design and implementation
4. Quality management

Each phase consists of several processes necessary to generate the desired results (Figure 5).

Project Initiation

- Create the process
- Manage risk
- Produce estimates
- Allocate resources
- Plan for continuous improvement
- Devise the system proposal

Requirements and Specifications

- Identify needs
- Elicit requirements
- Gather requirements
- Prioritize requirements
- Analyze requirements
- Manage requirements

Design and Implementation

- Generate application architecture
- Generate application databases
- Design interfaces
- Create code
- Integrate
- Document

Quality Management

- Create a test

- Develop procedures
- Execute tests
- Report results
- Conduct user acceptance testing (UAT)
- Prepare retrospectives

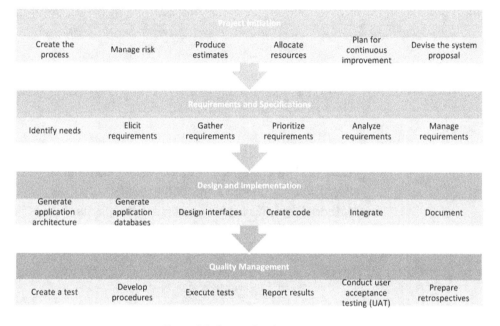

Figure 5 Software development

Each part contributes in some way to the overall software creation. Though not all building blocks are equally important, they are all needed to have valid, functional software.

The software development process calls for dividing the development into stages to produce the desired software package per stakeholder requirements. Software development is not a straight path. Sometimes you must backtrack to get the desired product. The process is but one step in a larger schema to deliver results—from activities to methodology.

Here is a quick overview of the software development process to jump-start your knowledge. Let's start with basic definitions:

- **Task**: This is a specific piece of work carried out under instruction.
- **Activity**: This is a group of related tasks. The activity is linked to a role (the person who executes each task) and the resources needed to perform the activity.

Figure 6 *Activity main ingredients*

- **Process**: This is the task flow.
- **Practices**: These are a set of processes like continuous integration/continuous delivery (CI/CD).
- **Methodology**: This is a group of practices. (Scrum is an example.)

Figure 7 *Definitions hierarchy*

The Software Team

It's a mistake to expect software developers to conduct an entire development cycle. Many software developers will stretch out original tasks to cover for a shortfall. At the end of the process, the application must be more than just coding. There are too many moving parts to rely solely on software developers to create an effective system for customers and users.

Usually, any given application consists of at least of these elements:

- Application
  - Content
  - Application data
- User interface (UI)
  - Logos
  - Colors
  - Buttons
- Programming
  - Layout
  - Code
- Documentation
  - User manual
  - Application documentation

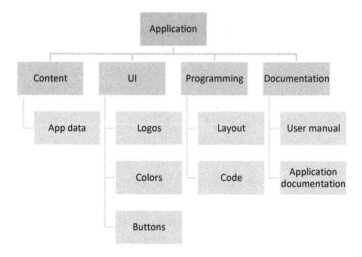

Figure 8 Application building blocks

Five main roles will be linked to the application requirements. Some will require subordinate roles if the project is very large:

- Project manager (PM)
- Business analyst (BA)
- Developer
- Quality tester
- UI developer

Each plays a crucial role. Sometimes, these roles will change depending on the project. But the roles usually will align properly with system development processes. Ideally, someone should be designated to oversee the overall process and activities to ensure functioning software.

Figure 9 Project team roles

The most confusing role is that of the developer. Depending on the project size, developer capabilities may extend to business analysts, developers, and quality testers. The development may take on only one role or all three. In any case, developer tasks will be to:

- Design the database
- Develop the database
- Create the input fields on the user interface
- Determine the code to match the logic
- Create the documentation for these features
- Write tests for these features
- Run tests for these features

Usually, there are additional roles hidden among the developer tasks and the databases. For a small project, the developer usually takes these on. A database architect should ensure the databases are built correctly for a complex system.

Development Life Cycle

Let's consider the example of a modern, generic development life cycle. The cycle starts at the source code and extends to the final work and production value delivery. Following are the common elements in the development life cycle. Though these vary from team to team, the overall concept is the same:

Source code repository, a version control system for tracking changes (like GIT).

Build systems, systems that watch the source code repository and alert you when a new build is required (like Jenkins).

Build tool, a tool that orchestrates and compiles (like Dockers for build and Kubernetes for orchestration). The same applies to programming languages.

Test, a test should be fast (done in under five minutes), reliable, and able to isolate failures. It should provide feedback. The initial types of testing are:

- **Unit testing**: This tests individual components (class or subsystem). The developer typically conducts it to confirm the code is functioning. (70% of tests)
- **Integration testing**: This tests groups of subsystems (collections of subsystems) and, eventually, an entire system. The developer typically does this test. (20% of tests)

At this point, you have a build with associated test results. These are called *artifacts*. If a test failed, it would not become an artifact. Artifacts follow the same version control process as the source code.

Building the server: To build the server and deploy the build into the production or preproduction environment, you will perform:

- Integration testing
- System testing
- UI (end-to-end testing)
- Security testing
- Performance testing
- Acceptance testing

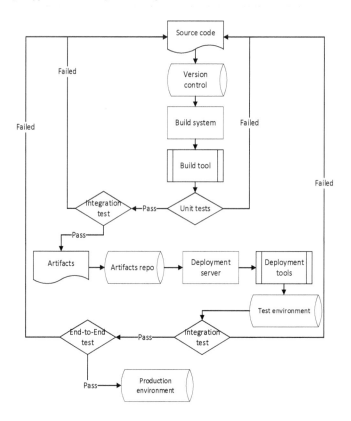

Figure 10 Development life cycle

Production deployment: Use the same deployment tool and build that you used in your development environment to deploy to production.

I always recommend separating the preproduction from production. When testing a new build, it's always best to either clone production machines or restores from a recent backup.

Once you finalize the realization to production, the cycle starts all over again for a new feature. This is what's called the *product version* or *building the road map*, and to do so, you need to work in multiple directions simultaneously. If you have an application with 10 features, it's not possible to do it in serial, so usually, it's done in a parallel manner, and that's what's called *branching code*.

Branching Codes

Branching codes are a tool developers use to create features and fixes. The code branches are necessary to deliver value. Though there is no magic bullet in branching, successful branching should not live long and should be integrated into the main branch.

Start with a developed product based on the customer's stated requirements. This becomes version 1.0. When you discover a bug, create a fix and release master version 1.1.

Additional features are developed in the sub-feature branch. Integrate both the new features and the fixes released to patch version 1. When you create a new version in the master branch, it becomes version 2. This is only a snapshot. But you repeat the process by getting a new requirement for development, mixing it with the old code, then releasing a new version.

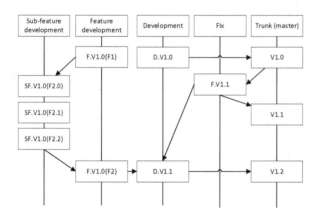

Figure 11 Branching codes

Each software branch has a separate timeline for development and usually has different practices applied to it. But in the end, the code will be integrated into one main branch.

Creating the Code

Coding is all about writing code, and it's the longest phase of the entire project (even with Agile), so it's best to highlight a few things

Programming language: There is no best coding language; almost all languages can be used to solve problems. But some will solve problems with much less code than others. It's very difficult to change the language after the coding starts.

Framework: A set of prewritten code to simplify the writing process. A framework is built using one or many programming languages. Most frameworks will cost more than coding from scratch although the overall cost will be reduced due to time saved and quality improvement.

Low-code/no code: A new emerging technology that utilizes a graphical interface to build a solution faster, though the cost is more expensive, and the development options are usually limited. If the business is pressing to find a solution, sometimes it's best to fulfill some of the use cases using a low/no-code solution and then take the time to build a more feature-rich system. Usually, it takes 10% of the time to build the same solution on a low-code system. In other words, you can finish software that normally would be coded in a year in six weeks.

Software pattern: This is a predefined way to get the code to perform a specific function using standard terminology, syntax, and definitions. The primary reason for using it is to reduce code complexity and improve the overall coding structure. And sometimes it may provide solutions to problems you faced previously. So, before you try to solve a problem using a new method, try to find a pattern for it first. Patterns come in all levels of software.

Refactoring: Refine code design to make it extensible, clean, and easy to understand. Usually, this happens when quality control is skipped for the benefit of time or economic constraints, leading to technical debt. The fewer best practices and quality controls used, the slower the changes will be. And the difficulty of adding new features will double with each new feature, causing software development to slow to a total stop until the code is refactored.

Clean code/spaghetti code: These two terms are used to define how easily another person reads the code without direct instruction and how easy it is to extend or modify the code. To turn spaghetti code into clean code, you perform refactoring, and the team uses patterns to define the structure. Sometimes, clean code turns into spaghetti code due to time or budget pressure. The idea is not to leave it in the spaghetti state for long and refactor it as fast as possible.

Chapter 2: Identify and Elicit Requirements

....

You will always hear that Agile is light on documentation. This is partially true. As you go along, you gradually build the documentation; each document is a few pages long and created to serve a specific purpose. Usually, the project will follow one standard of project management. And this project management method will require creating particular documents as deliverables. But the building blocks will remain the same.

Requirements gathering, collections, or similar terms usually refer to the product's general requirements and specifications. The actual requirements are the same across methods. But the collections come as one big document in Waterfall and smaller chunks for Agile. Both approaches have pros and cons. Generally, the requirements and specification process goes through specific phases regardless of the methodology. The methodology will dictate only how deeply you will drill down into each one. The process typically consists of the following:

- **Identifying needs**: Identify the vision and the strategy of the project.
- **Eliciting requirements**: This is where the interviews and working with the stakeholders come into play. Use focus groups and individual interviews to understand the needs.
- **Gathering requirements**: Rephrase the requirements into a solid statement and validate it with users.
- **Prioritizing requirements**: Begin establishing some priorities. In other words, arrange the requirements and quantify the relative importance of these needs.
- **Analyzing requirements**: Ensure they are complete, clear, and consistent with the other requirements and measurable data. Write the needs in a meaningful way and identify latent needs.

- **Managing requirements**: Categorize the requirements, code them for reference, and change the management process later.

Though these are the major steps required to identify the requirements, these activities are not all that is needed. Usually, during an Agile project, course correction is the only certainty. Sometimes, even the team will need to do code refactoring. The idea is to ensure that this happens as minimally as possible. So, the first part is to determine where the business is now and where the business wants to go, and where the project fits into the whole or fills part of a gap.

The business analyst has become more of a product manager. They are the link between the users, sponsors, customers, the developer, and all SME teams. The BA/PM constantly translates between the customer's business request and the SME team's technical requirements. You will need to communicate so that both teams will clearly understand each other. Getting a group of people to agree on something can be quite challenging. In a typical setup, the BA/PM will be commissioned by someone to work on a project and directed to someone else, usually a manager representing your customer group. After a short discussion, they would redirect the workshop to one or more of their subordinates. At this point, either they gather the requirements directly from those individuals, or they gather more individuals in a meeting to provide them with the requirements.

This setup involves no stakeholder discovery or uncovering of any issues. In most cases, the ones who will actually use the system are not the ones that will provide you with the majority of the requirements, which means you are building a system for the wrong stakeholder group. In such a case, the system will get many comments after it goes live. To avoid this scenario, the first step is to determine the current system versus the to-be system.

If the customer organization is already a running operation, some system will already be in place. You need to know what the users like and dislike about the current system. This will make the project much easier down the road. Don't accept responses like "We need the same system but faster." Usually, such vague requests have many underlying reasons. So, explore what they mean. Faster response (server and code)? Faster operations (UX design)? Or faster output (DB, query, and reporting)? Why are they building a new system instead of tweaking the existing one? These questions will open the door to investigating more solutions and bring greater insights. The individuals who will provide these insights are currently fulfilling these functions—leading to more accurate requirements gathering.

On rare occasions, the new system will replace bad practices and enforce governance in some aspects; still, you need to highlight such bad practices and the new practices that the new system is trying to achieve. Try to document the existing system and why it's being replaced by something else since bad practices seem to resurface from time to time. All requirements usually are listed in *software requirements specification* (SRS) or system requirement documents. Both mean the same thing. It is a specification describing the software to be developed, including functional and nonfunctional requirements. The term came from before the Agile concept, and it is still in use, but it's accepted that such a document will have multiple versions, and additional information is added or removed with each version. In addition to whatever sprint tracking software provides, this document is a deliverable. You will have to track all aspects of the sprint and the overall project in this document.

The main issue in large projects is that the business analyst often doesn't get back to users quickly because they don't have access to the users/customers, have nothing more to add, or can't make a decision. This may lead to assumptions by the developer that can result in misalignment between the customer vision and the application delivered.

In other words, such assumptions might require some clarification in the future or even code refactoring. A project requiring only three months may take six to eight months due to poor requirements definition and the need for rework. The cost of that rework can be

50 percent more than the estimated cost. And about 85 percent of the rework cost may come from requirements errors. That would leave 15 percent of requirements changes due to changing environmental conditions and business needs during the project.

The issue with gathering all requirements in one shot is that the customer doesn't think about the entire process, and change requests may come later, in waves. One way of addressing this is to create throwaway prototypes and minimum viable product (MVP) to walk the customer through the process. There is nothing wrong with accommodating customer requirements even after project delivery, but it's important to close the gap as much as possible so that the rework and assumptions are minimal.

To aid the process, set the users' expectations by arranging to meet with them around five times to collect requirements. This will happen in rounds because each answer you receive will generate more questions, so plan this before the first meeting. Depending on the number of users, I recommend doing this in one-to-one sessions (at least three meetings with three different users) and conducting at least two workshops with a group of users. Preferably, conduct the workshops first for faster requirement gathering and then plan the one-to-one sessions. Though the number of stakeholders is small, they are essential, which will be discussed later in the stakeholder section.

This simple approach will allow you to collect 70 percent of the requirements in a week, and then you will spend the remainder of your time fine-tuning the requirements. The initial 70 percent will allow a better plan of how things will look. It will also allow you to build the business's and users' requirements and develop the functional and nonfunctional requirements. Though there is still a risk of 30% unknown requirements, this is usually the best option versus the waste of time and cost from not performing a high-level design or process optimization earlier. If the project did include these steps, the changes will be due to clarification, fine-tuning, environmental changes, and business direction.

Users typically can't express what they like, but they can spot what they don't like and articulate it very well. Another critical consideration is that users prefer an inferior product they know how to use over a superior product they don't know how to use. So, take time to study the old systems to ensure the new system will be intuitive to the users and reduce adoption resistance. Also, business culture plays a major role in what's acceptable and what's not in terms of colors and how items look and feel. So, don't underestimate the power of the design. This will be the first thing the user/customer sees, and it generates an instant reaction.

Identify Needs

To identify the project's vision or strategy, you need to scope it first. You may wish to identify needs for the entire application or the system. Either way, you want the client to be thinking about the system's goals. Usually, you get these from the sponsor and the project/program manager.

Identify your primary agents—the user, the administrator, the system, the server, and so on—and who will engage with each facet. Typically, you build a high-level organization chart in the first workshop. This will give you an idea of who you should ask if you need specific information.

This is critical since you are building while the team is working, so you must constantly provide requirements to maintain the project. So, to identify the need correctly, you will need to identify three levels of objectives for the project:

- **Strategic:** from the management
- **Operational:** from the middle management
- **Tactical:** from whoever is working on the system

And to identify the need from each level, you need first to identify two aspects:

- **The organization**: Determine how the new system fits into the existing structure. This is to identify the context of the overall systems.

- **The stakeholders**: Identify the groups that will provide the needed information.

If you don't know enough about the organization, the first step will be to conduct a content study.

Build Organizational Context

The content study objective is to gain a deep understanding of the organization in order to have a better context when asking the questions and collecting the requirements. It's divided into three main phases.

Phase One

What was the history of the current system? And why was it built the way it is? Create a system–responsibility matrix that identifies every user responsible for the current system and the system's primary users.

Note: The word *system* does not necessarily mean a software system; it's the transformation process from input to output. It could include software systems and manual activities.

An ideal scenario is to have a swimlane chart showing the entire process with each activity owner. If not, at least you need to build a block-based process and identify the performer of each activity.

Phase Two

Start reading to understand the company's background, organization chart, business plans, policy manuals, financial reports, meeting minutes, and job descriptions.

Phase Three

Build an understanding of how the system functions. Read books, training materials, articles, and regulations in the domain. Also, ask about two key areas:

- **The artifacts**: Up-to-date information about the current system and preexisting documents, drawings, storyboards, prototypes, and so on.

- **The stakeholders**: All parties affected by the new system.

Stakeholders Discovery

A stakeholder typically is anyone who might be impacted by the project positively or negatively. Stakeholders usually are:

- **Sponsor**: These are the entities paying for the solution, and they may derive the most benefit from the project. The sponsor could be a single person or a group of people, but usually they are referred to singularly as *the sponsor*. If you have multiple groups of people, then use the plural *sponsors*.
- **Customers or buyers**: This group will decide to accept or reject the solution. The group can be a subset of the sponsor or an entirely different entity.
- **Users**: The user group comprises those who will use the product daily. This group has subcategories:
  - **Primary users** will use the product, initially built for them, daily.
  - **Secondary users** occasionally use the product and usually need to know how it functions, but they are not deeply involved.

The first step in stakeholder discovery is to create the new swimlane diagram showing the new process of the system, or at least the block-based process, with owners. This group will be your primary group of stakeholders. Afterward, create a stakeholder diagram showing who has a relationship with the application and who determines the product design (primary owner). The diagram also will detail the relationship between the primary owner and other entities. This simple context will provide insights into the use cases required.

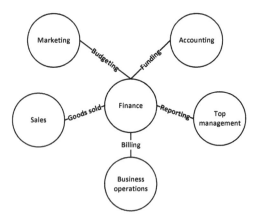

Figure 12 Stakeholder diagram

Finding Additional Stakeholders

To find additional stakeholders, you need to grasp the "funnel" concept. The funnel is very common in sales and marketing. It says the volume you put in differs from what you get out.

The difference depends on the industry and the user engagement level within an organization. But generally, if you contact 100 users, only 60 will respond. Out of these 60, only 24 will be interested in moving forward. The others will simply apologize or will have scheduling issues. And out of those 24, you may have only eight people interested in proceeding with the interview.

You need at least seven people to identify requirements correctly, and you need 14 to cover all the bases. Some participants will specialize in the roles you have already researched. But since you need to cover a wide range of various roles and departments, you can accept a few people with duplicate job descriptions.

The maximum number of people you should interview within a single role is three. Any more than that, and you will be wasting time. Try to ensure you are interviewing people evenly dispersed throughout the organization. Under the funnel concept, note that you must contact many users and stakeholders to get the desired interview pool. Occasionally, issue mass announcements to the entire organization, and send personalized emails afterward to boost participation.

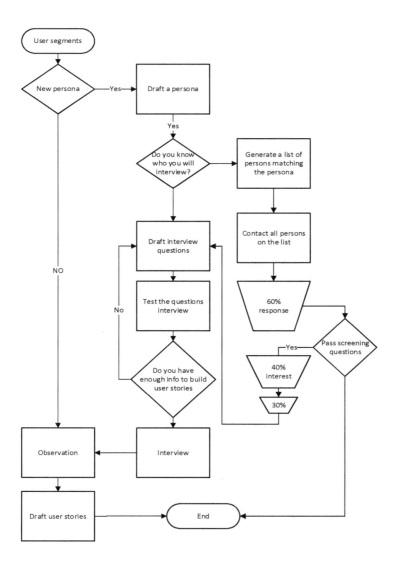

Figure 13 *Overall process*

To define the needed use cases or edge cases (use cases that do not happen very often), you need to broaden the search to discover more individuals. But having such a large group of stakeholders will be an obstacle. It will help if you can determine how to get the maximum benefits while keeping the number of involved parties as minimal as possible. In such a case, follow this filtration approach:

Step 1: Start with questionnaires (multiple-choice or weighted questions scaled from 1 to 10 or 1 to 5 with blank space under each question for notes).

Step 2: Send these questions to a large group of people (maybe the entire employee group) with a specific deadline of a week if the survey takes five minutes to complete. The results should fall into one of these categories:

- **Group A**: The largest group queried will offer no response.
- **Group B**: Some will respond with the basic information but add no comments.
- **Group C**: Some will respond with answers and include comments on some or all questions.

Interviewing respondents in group C is critical to get their points of view. But identifying the group C respondents won't be easy when small groups are queried because response rates tend to be low. For example, you can expect a response rate of 1% to 1.5%. If you send queries to 10 people, none may respond. Or some may reply, but not from group C. Instead, send the questionnaires to 100 people, and you might get two responses. So, this method tends to work most effectively with larger groups.

The objective will be to interview about seven stakeholders from group C to gain their insights into the new system. These users will complement the overall solution by helping identify additional system needs.

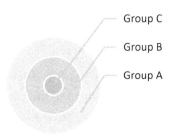

Group C

Group B

Group A

Figure 14 User groups

You now have the group of key users (the seven core users) you need to go forward. Contact them personally, preferably face-to-face or by phone, to seek their participation. Otherwise, your project will have missed some requirements without those core users. Any additional interested user or stakeholder will go through the funnel to ensure they can pass the screening and are the correct person to interview.

Group Stakeholders Based on Interest

The users you are getting to know are not one homogeneous group. Typically, they represent a mix of multiple interests. For example, marketing and finance will have two distinct subgroups, each with independent and overlapping interests. Track those differences by segmenting the groups into personas. Creating a persona is engaging during a workshop (and builds rapport with you). And it's far more engaging than placing/referring to people as being from group A or B. You will need to create one or more personas for each segment, a process that will give a face to your efforts.

Note: Creating a persona for a new product is a must. While it can also benefit more limited projects, such as product updates, it is not imperative in those instances.

Step 1: Create a Face

Start by imagining one or more of your groups and giving each a face. Don't use actual photos. The website https://thispersondoesnotexist.com/ will generate an image for you based on AI. You can refresh the page until you see an image representing your imagined persona. Try to differentiate the choices by making at least three personas.

Step 2: Create a Profile

- Give each a name. It will make for easier meetings.

- Describe the details of each group, such as level of education, likes or dislikes, career choices, and preferred technology.
- To create a simple biography, you need to answer four questions:
    - What is their motivation?
    - Where do they spend their time?
    - How do they spend their time?
    - Why might they be interested in the product?

For example:

Name: Alex
Age: 23–43
Gender: Male
Interests: Fitness and wellness, shopping and fashion, outdoor sports, technology
Education level: College graduate
Job title: Financial advisor or analyst
Income: 40K to 80K
Relationship status: Married
Language spoken: English, French
Buying motivation: He wants to stand out in a work environment.
Buying concerns: He is price-conscious and responds well to sales and discounts.

These biographies will become the bases for discussions with two types of users:

Internal: These are business users who work inside the company. You can go through the chain of command to ensure their cooperation and participation in the information gathering.

External: These are not-yet-identified individuals who will use your system (a mobile ordering app, for example) and can give feedback. Drawing out these customers requires perseverance and a tolerance for rejection. You'll need to go where these users might congregate, introduce yourself, explain briefly that you are doing research, and ask for a few minutes to get their input. Up to 90 percent of the external candidates may ignore you or decline the request. But responses from the remaining 10 percent can help you a great deal.

The Application Audience

The most challenging application is one that tries to solve multiple problems at once and deliver functions for more than one group of users. This isn't easy since the techniques of collecting information differ from one group to another. Though the idea is the same across audiences, there is some variation in control over the parties involved and the ability to get them to disclose their requirements.

Figure 15 Application audience

Usually, I have found that the internal company employees are the most accessible group for discovering the requirements. Next are partners and suppliers since you can arrange a meeting with their purchasing department.

The two most challenging groups are B2B and B2C customers.

In the case of B2B, you can interview only the existing business customers. It's quite challenging to interview a business you are not dealing with due to lots of confidential information that both parties would have to disclose. However, In B2C customers, you will have some more tactics to collect the requirements. The challenging part is to get people to talk to you.

Requirements Elicitation

Requirements elicitation means getting the correct requirements from users by asking the right questions. You need a solid knowledge of the system in question and the organization to ask the correct questions. Many techniques for eliciting insights will aid an Agile or similar process. Among the most effective:

- Workshops (work best in internal setup)
- Interviews (work across all audiences)
- User stories (used with other methods)
- Scenarios (used with other methods)
- Negative requirements (used with other methods)
- Prototyping and MVP (work best with external users)

But before exploring each of these methods, two things need distinction—the *needs* and the *wants*. Be sure you know the difference during the requirements gathering. If the budget is tight, wants will be eliminated first, then specific types of needs.

Want: The desired function the customer wants to see in the product.

Need: A core function required to address a specific issue or solve a particular problem. Sometimes, the needs are referred to as *pain*, and typically fall into one of three types:

- **Current pain**: A problem the customer recently discovered and is trying to solve. This is important to the current project.
- **Latent pain**: A problem that has existed so long that users have learned to live with it daily or have found a way to work around it. These latent problems are likely to be discovered only by watching the user work with the system for some time. After observing the users using the system, a few odd observations will be identified. For example, if the browser doesn't load the system, the user must keep hitting refresh to load the page. This is important to the customer but might be addressed in another project if there is a budget limitation.
- **Possible pain**: A problem the customer will have in the future if they do not act on it in the present. This will mostly be pushed to another phase of the project or a different project entirely.

Workshops

Workshops are an effective method of collecting requirements, and usually the first interaction with a group. These require a solid structure to avoid wasting workshop time. Once you have identified the stakeholders, you will work closely with them to determine the requirements. Around seven to 12 people, including the sponsor, will be required to attend the workshops. The workshops will be useful for more than requirements gathering, so they should be scheduled throughout the project. If you are building a new product, you'll need about seven, plus or minus two. The required number of workshops could be three if you are replacing an existing system. These sessions should adhere to the following structure:

1. **Brainstorm**: Build on the ideas of others without judgment.
2. **Explore potential solutions**: Explore how the different parts can come together.
3. **Vote**: Practice open voting—everyone can vote up to three times, and no votes are private.
4. **Conduct a model selection session**: For example, Sketch modeling or modeling of interface concepts
5. **Use an alpha prototype**: This can be a digital prototype or rough version that looks and acts like the final. Such a prototype is derived from techniques distinct from what you might otherwise select to produce a final product. In other words, many corners are cut.
6. **Test concept**.
7. **Conclude**.

The most important session or sessions involve brainstorming. if you do not get this right, every step that follows will be impacted. Generally, the purposes of the exploration and brainstorming workshop are:

- To intimately understand stakeholders' needs, emotions, desires, and problems
- To identify all stakeholders
- To understand and develop empathy
- To discover possible latent needs

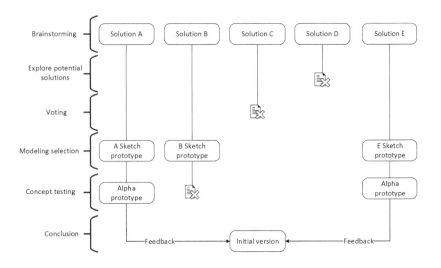

Figure 16 *Workshop structure*

Top Three Workshop Mistakes

There are a lot of mistakes that could happen in a workshop. But these three are the three you should always be mindful of since they tend to occur without you or anyone noticing:

- **Talking directly about an idea or a solution**: If you talk about an idea, the customer you are interviewing, hoping to help you, may tell you what you want to hear, not actual requirements.
- **Asking a leading question**: An example would be asking if the customer likes the color blue. The answer will be either yes or no . Instead, ask what colors the customer likes.
- **Going a mile wide and an inch deep**: Don't ask too many questions or dominate the conversation. Always try to make it a two-way conversation, with most of the talking from the customer side.

Interviews

Interviews usually mean one-to-one interviews or, in some cases, one-to-many, for example, if the entire family is considered one customer for the new application. But Building a new application will differ than if you replace an internal system. in both cases you can interview many types of user/customer groups. Here are the main three:

- **Internal users**: Users who work in the organization, as identified in earlier steps.
- **Regular people**: Individuals, often in locations that attract customer group members if you are building a new public application.
- **Paid users** (on Craigslist or Fiverr): Pay can range from $50 to $100 per interview for specialized people or less for mainstream users.

Interview Types

There are three types of interviews:

Internal meeting: This is a prescheduled meeting with one or more internal employees, and the major challenge is scheduling time slots.

Intercept: Wherever there is a line of random people linked in some fashion to your research, seek them out. If you are making a takeout application or "click to pick" application for coffee, approach a line of people waiting for takeout or their morning coffee. They may be frustrated, but they are stuck in line and may be willing to talk. You may have one to five minutes to hear about a customer's experience. That translates to one or two questions. So, you may ask, "What is your expectation related to X? And how is it currently performing?"

Another trick I have found useful with the younger generation is the YouTuber approach. People are somehow used to someone with a camera recording an interview for their YouTube channel. So, what does the trick is for the interviewer and someone holding the camera to approach the potential user and say, "We are building a new application. Are you willing to answer three questions for 20 dollars?" This typically gives you three to five questions and might even open the possibility for a scheduled extension.

The final approach, though unpredictable, is running a Facebook ad for your target group; whoever wishes to contribute will list their contact information.

Scheduled extension: This could be prescheduled or someone you met in an intercept willing to give you more information (paid or free). The usual duration for this interview is 30 minutes.

Interview Questions

The key in interviews is to start with general questions and gradually elicit answers with greater specificity as the interview progresses. Avoid asking leading questions. Try to make sure your early questions are general and open-ended, and your later questions are detailed as you press for more specific responses. Following is an example of an intercept type interview for a restaurant that wants to evaluate whether to create an online ordering application (web or mobile). In this case, the initial question put to customers might look like this:

"Tell me about yourself as a customer. What motivates you to come to the restaurant?"

This preliminary question will have two effects. It will build rapport and open the door to questions of motivation. After the initial query, you should drill a bit deeper, guiding the customer to the question of how they might order a meal. You might ask:

- How did you decide to come to the restaurant instead of ordering by phone?
- What are your thoughts about mobile ordering applications and food delivery services?
- What do you think is good and bad about X?
- How do you usually order food from a restaurant? How many times a month do you place a takeout food order by phone? Via an online app? How often do you use food delivery services?

Usually, these are the essential questions for the first round. Later, you will refine your questions based on the feedback and the ideas you collected from the initial interviews. It takes three small rounds of interviews to get the questions right.

It's always helpful to refine the questions in organizational settings by conducting mock interviews. In other words, ask your colleagues your questions to get a feel for the interview flow and get feedback about your approach.

You may have noticed that all the questions mentioned are intended to help you understand what's valuable and what's not. This process helps if you're thinking about a system and want to explore its potential success with internal or external users.

If you work in an organizational environment and the application audience is internal or professional users, the interview approach will remain the same, though you won't need to intercept someone. In such a setting, you arrange a meeting with a clear agenda, even if you plan to implement an ERP system. The questions and ideas will remain the same, starting with general questions about motivation and the process and getting to specifics later in the discussion. The idea behind these questions is to challenge the system's value and avoid wasting resources on unnecessary items.

Over time, unnecessary items can choke the system because they were never essential. Rather, they were costly because someone had to implement them and integrate them into the process. Always evaluate the value of a given item and then decide what you need and don't need.

During the Interview

- Avoid leading questions. Instead, funnel questions in sequence from general to specific.
- Don't ask why.
- Don't ask yes/no questions.
- Don't interrupt the flow or direction of the interview.
- Don't jump on a specific problem if you discover one.
- Circle back to an earlier topic if you need added depth.
- Be willing to explore topics that the interviewee brings up.

Improving the Quality of the Interview

This step usually is arranged before an interview and can give you an early look at an interviewee's routine.

- **Diary study**: Give participants diaries and ask that they record their actions and feelings at a specific time or interval (like 9 a.m., noon, and 3 p.m. daily). Usually, you will craft different questions for this exercise. This feedback should proceed throughout the day in the same vein and structure. Videos or voice recorders also can help record actions and feelings.
- **Experience sampling**: You can also lay the groundwork for participants to receive pop-up calls or chats during the day to answer questions.

A simple mobile application that sends the subjects notifications periodically throughout the day can collect far more effective results. This reusable platform changes only the questions from one project to another to explore users' reactions.

User Stories

During an interview or a workshop, you can easily build what's called a *user story*. It's a simple functionality the users requested. It follows a simple format.

As a . . . I want to . . . so that I can . . .

User stories need not be long or complex. They can be as simple as

"As a data entry employee, I want the cursor to automatically move to the next box so that I can type continuously without using the mouse to click the text field."

A good story should be:

- **Independent**, with little or no reliance on other stories.
- **Negotiable**, so that some elements in the story can be changed or defined later if needed by the team.
- **Valuable** to the user.
- **Estimable**, meaning that the developer can estimate the effort required (story points).

- **Small**, meaning that it should have few points.
- **Testable**, so it can be tested and marked as done.

To generate user stories, you can usually conduct one of three options:

User story writing workshop: Perform a user analysis and create a user group persona if needed. Let everyone write their stories based on the functionality desired in the application. Once you collect all this, start grouping stories into themes or epics. This workshop is very free-form, though I have found it stressful for many users/customers.

Spikes: These are knowledge-gathering stories to test a hypothesis. The stories are used for exploratory research work. It's usually timeboxed (five days or something similar) and has a clear definition of *done*. Usually, the spike output is thrown away. It's used to build knowledge and test something. It can be considered similar to prototyping.

Story mapping: This method is the easiest way to generate user stories. Stories are derived by tracking the chronological steps a user takes, starting with opening the application and progressing through its functionality. You will map this process from the top down, beginning with the activities and user actions. Then you can use this map to plan the stories.

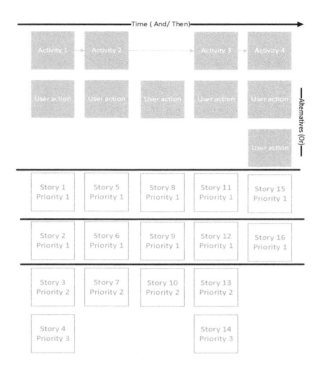

Figure 17 Story mapping

Storyboarding

Storyboarding seems too much effort for many, so it is often avoided. But storyboarding doesn't have to be complex. You can use simple stick figures to draw it. An entire storyboard should take no more than an hour to create, and it's a great communication tool.

Storyboarding is used in the movie industry. It's like a comic strip showing how a story or situation may progress toward a final result. Usually, it's used to demonstrate user interactions with other elements like a prototype or mockup to highlight a specific situation, such as a customer registration or new order.

It is employed when endpoint users are different from those you are talking to. For example, suppose you are building an e-commerce site to sell a product, and you don't have access to the final users or potential customers. In that case, you can use storyboarding to visualize these customers.

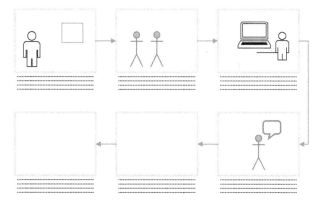

Figure 18 Storyboard

You can apply page linking and use wireframes to demonstrate the pages and how they link together. For a seamless presentation, choosing a compatible look and feel for all pages is good before mapping them to one another.

Scenarios

Imagine two or more paths for users and develop a scenario for each—for example, a happy or sad path, or a best-case/worst-case scenario. These paths will become tools for discovering solutions. They represent the worst possible way a solution could function and still be acceptable and the best possible way to function. Creating boundaries in the use cases. To have a valid scenario, you need:

- What
- Who
- When
- How

Through this process, you will define how a:

- Happy path = normal scenario = positive outcome
- Sad path = abnormal scenario = negative outcome

You may have other definitions based on your cases, so you should create definitions for each of them. These scenarios also help in writing test cases.

As previously mentioned, users are quite good at articulating what they don't want. *Negative requirements* are the requirements that should generate an error if they occur. When writing the scenarios, you will find that some scenarios are implicit, and no one made them explicit. You will want to cite them clearly in the requirements document. The scenarios fall into one of three categories:

- **Known, known**: These are very clear requirements received from a stakeholder.
- **Known, unknown**: This may be an implicit requirement received but not explicitly listed as a requirement. (This calls for making some assumptions.)
- **Unknown, unknown**: These are the requirements no one has implicitly or explicitly mentioned but still are required. An example might be a log-in screen. No one will ask for it, but it's assumed it's required. The same is true for access. Generally, all types of security requirements are considered implicit and unknown.

Identify these security requirements and write down any assumptions about them.

	What	Who	When	How	
Open the system	The meeting system	Any users	9 a.m. to 6 p.m.	By web portal	Positive
Open the system	The meeting system	Any users	6 p.m. to 8 a.m.	By web portal	Negative
System override	The meeting database	Admin users	N/A	By web portal	Positive
System override	The meeting database	General users	N/A	By web portal	Negative

Table 1 Negative requirement

Chapter 3: Prototype as a Requirement Gathering Tool

....

A prototype is an approximation of the product or service. It is created to explore some aspects of the final product and ensure it matches the requirements and end-user specifications. Using complete prototypes as information collection tools is considered an extreme measure used only in uncertain situations under specific conditions, such as where you:

- Have only a business problem (business pain) *and*
- You don't know what the customer wants (and the customer doesn't know either or can't articulate) *and/or*
- Time is a significant constraint, so you start without knowing what the final picture will look like *and/or*
- Value realization is needed very fast

So, in such a case, you start very small and build minimal steps to deliver the fastest possible value, and on the back end, the team:

- Keeps the things the customer liked in the original version
- Eliminates the things the customer disliked
- Refactors (rewrites code) for the things the customer desires to become more integrated into the solution

You need to generate the initial result and show it to the end customer to validate the overall understanding of what's been gathered.

You do the prototyping in a design sprint to speed up the process. A design sprint is a special sprint with the team's only objective being to generate requirements and a design. The whole team is working on it, and, usually, it takes one week to go through all of its phases.

This chapter further explores the concepts of design sprints and prototypes. Each type is used in uncertain conditions—when creating a new application or something from scratch.

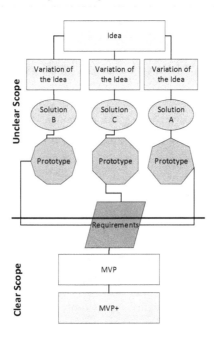

Figure 19 Uncertainty and scope

Executing the Sprint

In any given system, users may use only about 20 percent of the system daily. The remaining 80 percent is either used periodically or never (as in the case of packaged software). This means you can deliver business value from day-to-day operations from this 20 percent of usage. This is faster than developing the whole software product and waiting for the value to be achieved. Deciding on what parts to create and what to defer until later is carried out in the design sprint.

This design sprint approach was outlined in the book *Sprint: How to Solve Big Problems and Test New Ideas in Just Five Days* by Jake Knapp. The book primarily focuses on creating a high-fidelity design in a week, so integrating this method with prototyping for the entire software design across multiple layers, not just the interface, requires some adjustments.

The design sprint aims to identify who has what problem, and then the team works jointly to solve it. The design sprint is specially made to develop a prototype that can help clarify what's required. Before the design sprint, you need to know the answers to the following questions:

- Who is using the system (users)?
- What do we want to learn? How do our users deal with (problem areas)?
- Why we would like (the idea) plus improvement.
- What are the expected deliverables from this sprint?

The next step is to examine whether our value proposition is the best fix for a specific problem. Is it any better than the existing solutions? Are users motivated to use it? If not, how might they be motivated to use it?

The design sprint lays the groundwork for you to go to the customer with the ideas generated in the brainstorming workshops and query them on their likes and dislikes.

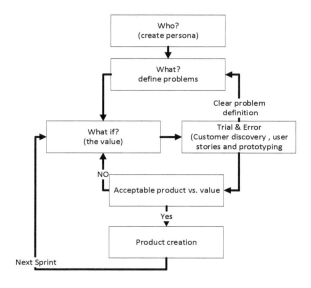

Figure 20 Design sprint

Full/native prototyping is another way to identify requirements and explore solutions. By showing users some simple products, you can pinpoint additional features and requirements to enhance the product further. Although this seems more practical than the design sprint, it costs more money and time. So, by combining the two (design sprints and prototypes), you generate the maximum value with the lowest cost.

Try first to launch the minimum viable product to collect feedback. Remember, you are exploring interaction with that 20 percent of the product users rely on for their day-to-day activities. The MVP will represent only about five percent of the full product. People usually overestimate their MVP. Start with what you think is the MVP, but realize that only about 25 percent of that is likely to be the actual MVP.

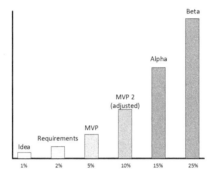

Figure 21 Features progress

Always do the prototypes in cycles, which typically consist of four steps:

- Gather requirements
- Create a prototype
- Show it to users
- Get feedback

Figure 22 Design sprint and prototype cycle

Usually, you repeat this cycle until no more requirements are needed to achieve your MVP. At this stage, the prototype should also have the full approval of the users. Typically, this occurs in three to four cycles.

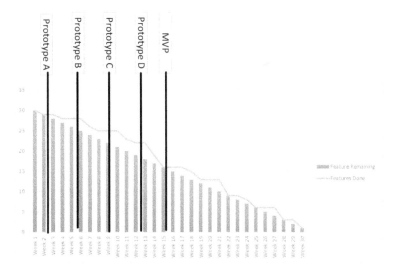

Figure 23 *Prototype and burn-down*

Please note that this is a working prototype, not just a model (drawing). In other words, you modify the product with each change, enhancing it further as the project progresses.

In the next section, let's explore prototyping and how it might benefit the project.

Prototyping to Realize the Value in Uncertain Conditions

Prototypes are divided into multiple groups based on the information collected. Generally, the three types of prototyping that would be of interest for a software project are:

- Sketching and paper prototype
- Digital prototype (sometimes called high-fidelity prototype)
- Native prototype

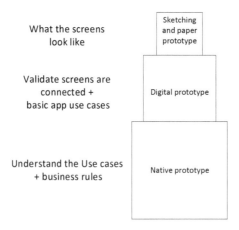

Figure 24 *Three levels of prototyping*

Usually, you start with the easiest (sketching and paper prototypes) and move to more advanced techniques during the project.

Sketching and Paper Prototype

The primary purpose of the paper prototype is to get an overall understanding of what the application's screens will look like and how many application screens are needed. In doing so, estimations of the effort required and the sprints can be made. This prototyping technique depicts the interfaces as they look to the end user. The sketch should evolve from a rough drawing to a realistic illustration.

Digital Prototyping

This means building an idea using digital interfaces to create an interactive experience for the user. We use digital-looking designs to ensure that the idea is the same for both the customer and the engineers working on it. This will give the prototype the same look and feel without building the actual software or final product. The outcome of digital prototyping is to understand some of the use cases and how the screens are linked together.

Native Prototyping

Native prototyping is a technique that builds the application using the fastest possible way to gather requirements. It uses real applications' data and is tested with a subset of users/customers.

People try to avoid this kind of prototype because it is very costly. We use it only if the customer is requesting something with many unknowns, such as unknown integration points, or a new product that did not exist before. It's used as a pilot to get better reactions from the customer as to what's needed. The code in this prototyping is used to demonstrate the functionality. In other words, the SMEs will be taking shortcuts and the shortest path possible, which means:

- No clean code
- Simple use case
- Simple architecture
- Few or no nonfunctional requirements
- Little or no quality assurance (QA)

As mentioned earlier, an MVP represents about 5% of the expected application uses, and the first prototype is about 1% to 2% of the overall uses; this would translate to one use case or two. This is to produce something that will function close to the expectation using everyday use cases. Afterward, fill in the special use cases and apply the best practices.

Native prototypes can be categorized by variances in the build method and the final prototype. There are four main types:

- **Exploratory**: Build the minimum code needed to make the product function and simulate the look and feel of the actual product, so it's mainly the "look and feel" but with some code behind it. Usually, this has some costs associated with it. It's recommended to do this to avoid costly rework down the road.
- **Throwaway**: The first version of the product helped you learn about the real requirements. You don't modify and reuse the code but start from scratch. In this case, this is called a *throwaway*.
- **Incremental**: Build the core features (the "must-have feature" to do the MVP) and add more and more features that enhance the product's functionality.
- **Evolutionary**: Divide the features by complexity and revise the features as you go along. In other words, start with a fully

functional system, but with not all options available. You will have the foundation for all features, but all will be labeled soon. Then start developing the components incrementally.

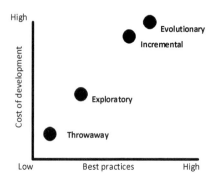

Figure 25 *Types of native prototypes*

Both evolutionary and incremental types overlap to some degree in real environments. The only difference between the two is that you don't know where you are heading in incremental, but you have a product road map in evolutionary.

Between both, you can even simplify further by mixing the product features. For example, do the "must-haves" in the simplest form (MVP) and then start advancing the features. Then add the "should haves" in the simplest way, and grow some more. Lastly, add the "nice to haves" in the simplest form, and grow again. This is a hybrid model, evolutionary–incremental.

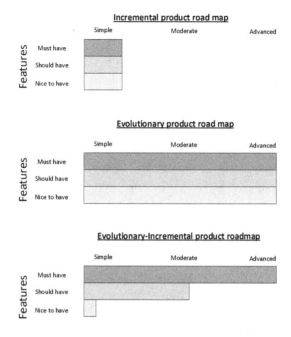

Figure 26 *Incremental, evolutionary, and evolutionary–incremental prototyping*

You could also build a basic foundation using the evolutionary–incremental approach for maximum flexibility and then add some exploratory features to be like throwaway, just to discover requirements and collect feedback. For the discovery process, you typically use throwaway prototypes.

Discover Requirements Using Prototypes

The *throwaway* is the product's first version that helped you discern the real requirements. You don't modify the first version. Instead, you toss it aside and continue the work by starting from scratch. One common advantage of the throwaway is failure mode identification. To identify the failure modes process, answer the following questions:

- The fastest route to failure is which method?
- If this product is going to fail, what will make it fail?
- What are the ways to reduce the failure mode?

After listing failure scenarios, expand on ways to avoid failure modes:

- Identify the failure modes
- Prioritize the failure modes
- Spend time on the most critical failure modes

Knowing what the customer dislikes usually provides insights into the software's motive and utility. This process is done using a real application and real data. This includes writing code in whatever language will be used. The code in this prototyping is used to demonstrate the function, so you will take shortcuts and seek the shortest path possible.

Unfortunately, this method always carries the greatest cost. It's typically used when there are difficulties in identifying the success criteria and the requirements. And we use paper and digital prototypes to avoid the cost of building a complete product at every stage of the discovery.

For example, the customer requests the team to build a chair. This is a business requirement with no additional specifications. Follow the process of trial and error to gather more requirements. And to reduce a specific type of uncertainty and reduce uncertainty in general, you can use many methods. The easiest way is to identify what they *don't* want first. Build things the team *knows* will fail somehow and test them to collect feedback on the actual requirements. This way, the customer will point out things they like and dislike. But don't start with something very far off the initial requirement to avoid customer frustration.

Figure 27 Requirements clarification using prototypes

In Figure 27, all chairs except for number 8 are considered throwaways.

Rapid Prototyping

Rapid prototyping is key to good solution design; something easy that can be made very quickly will help a great deal when building a product. Use a simple medium like paper or even 3-D printed objects. If the off-the-shelf software is used, it could be the exact system but on a very small scale and adjusted with little to no configuration.

Rapid prototyping refers to the speed at which you generate the prototypes—especially the very basic ones. The number of issues discovered when you try to build a cardboard prototype, or even a sketch, will give insight into what will work, what won't work, and some of the challenges you can expect. Rapid prototyping can be critical to an idea's success, reducing the time required to build the product.

Ideally, you will generate the ideas as quickly as possible to check their feasibility and ensure they are what the user wants. Typically, user feedback comes too late in the process. Rapid prototyping means building prototypes quickly and immediately showing them to end users. At this stage, end users will expect the product to be unpolished, so it's okay to reveal the rough elements of a product. And during prototype creation, you will discover ways to improve both the process and the product. It's an overall thinking exercise.

The prototype doesn't need to cover everything, but it needs to cover a specific product aspect. Ideally, it should replicate the whole product, but the time allowed and feedback usually require a much shorter cycle than waiting for a complete prototype. The trick is to generate ideas as quickly as possible, then check the idea's feasibility first and ensure this is what the user wants.

The biggest failure in a digital product is creating a product that doesn't solve an issue for the users, and adding unasked for features to it, assuming the user will like it more this way. Every idea generated needs to solve a need or a want for the customer group.

Stages of Requirements Discovery and User Feedback Capture

In prototyping, it's always "quantity over quality." Produce quickly, regardless of the quality, and learn from mistakes. In other words, you don't do just one when doing a wireframe. Instead, build three or more, let the customer select one, and tell you why they like it, and why they dislike the other ones. This articulation from the customer is one of the primary objectives of prototyping. The more variation you can make, the better. Though this is considered waste, wasting half a day at the start of the project is way better than wasting a month doing rework. The mistakes will accumulate quickly, leading to more adjustments to present progress. Focusing on prototype quality will result in one or two prototypes and not generate as many insights.

Prototyping can be performed in two ways, either serial or parallel. Try a mix of both to maximize efficiency. Start with many parallels (variations) and show them to the users. The next step is collecting feedback on which ones users liked better and why. Over time, try to incorporate all of these elements into one branch and perform more complex serial prototyping.

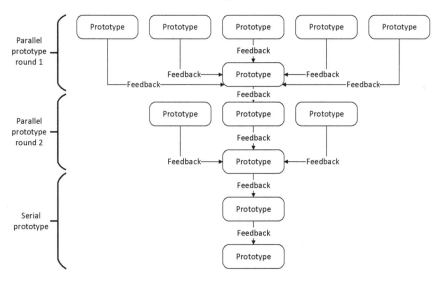

Figure 28 Prototype testing

Another critical aspect of having multiple prototypes is separating the ego from the actual feedback. If someone has one idea, it becomes their representation, and they won't accept criticism of it and will try to defend it and convince others of it's worth. But if there are multiple ideas, the team will learn more and become inclusive of all feedback. So, it's good to generate more ideas by asking the team to contribute to the concept before it becomes the main branch of the prototype.

Chapter 4: Gathering, Prioritizing, Analyzing, and Managing Requirements

You finished the requirements elicitation and clearly understood what the user group requires (utilizing any previous techniques, like interviews, workshops, and prototypes). It's time to move to the next phases of requirements engineering.

- **Gathering requirements**: Rephrasing the requirements into a solid statement and validating it with users.
- **Prioritizing requirements**: Begin establishing some priorities. In other words, arrange the requirements and quantify the relative importance of these needs.
- **Analyzing requirements**: Ensure they are complete, clear, and consistent with the other requirements and measurable data. Write the needs in a meaningful way and identify latent needs.
- **Managing requirements**: Categorize the requirements, code them for reference, and change the management process later.

Gathering Requirements

Gathering requirements calls for rephrasing them into a concrete statement and validating this with the users. When you initially finalize the elicitation, you will have many transcripts, notes, and ideas. In the gathering requirements phase, the aim is to consolidate these into a precise format. Gathering requirements consists of three main steps:

- Coding and categorizing
- Translation of the requirements
- Conflict analysis

Step 1: Coding and Categorizing

The starting point will be categorizing based on the type of requirement. There are two main types of requirements:

- **Functional requirements** or behaviors the product should perform or support. Usually, these follow a process format, with input, behavior, and output often shown in flow diagrams.
- **Nonfunctional requirements** could be the ease of navigating a user interface or the security of the product solution. These nonfunctional requirements can enable a product to perform well in a business environment. These can also be called *usability requirements*.

Within these two types, some requirements also might be tagged as:

- **Business requirements** define the business needs for the software project. This is the quantifiable business value. It should lay the groundwork for specific business goals. Here's an example.

  Provide faster shipping to our clients by reducing collecting and packaging time to under one hour from order placement.

  A business requirement is a product vision. Under business requirements, there typically are business rules. The rules can be divided into three categories:

  - **Budget**—such as the maximum budget to process each purchase order.
  - **Internal policies**—for example, all purchase orders should be approved by HR.
  - **Regulations**—the maximum withdrawal allowed from an ATM is $5000.

  Business rules are considered a constraint on how a product should function. They typically are not identified directly by users or stakeholders. They are usually discovered during the "process mapping."

- **User requirements** involve the tasks a user expects to perform with the software. (These are the "use cases.") User requirements include both functional and nonfunctional needs. But some defy categorization. In those cases, group them in the user requirements category.
- **External interfaces or external integration requirements** are requirements for a product being integrated with an external system.
- **Operational conditions requirements** can be needs like reliability and supportability. These factors, in turn, may be reliant on a physical object.

Technically, all requirements should be either functional or nonfunctional. But as technological innovations grow increasingly sophisticated, businesses need external interfaces to link to and receive connections from other services. This requires listing the operating conditions that will aid in developing an IoT (Internet of Things) communications solution. Usually, these kinds of projects have a related hardware component. In a smart city (typically within an urban area), the solution may be about 50/50—a fairly even split between hardware and software. In both instances, operating conditions are essential.

Through taxonomy, you will discover many requirement categories. The system does not need to cover all primary categories and subcategories. But the more requirements you compile, the larger the number of your subcategories.

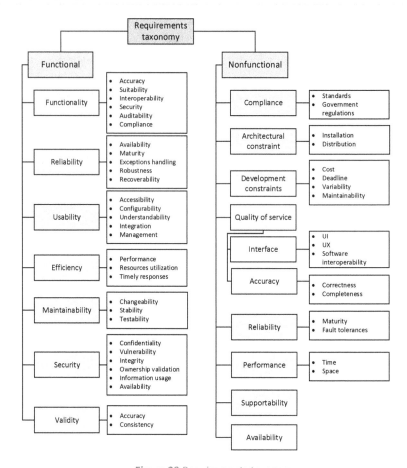

Figure 29 Requirements taxonomy

Coding the Requirements for Faster Tracking

Indexing these requirements and tracing them back to a specific user is important. There are two main steps:

(1) Assign a code to whatever you get from users. This could include artifacts, emails, PDF files, and so on. Whatever you include, be sure to assign it a code.

(2) Build the code matrix. Categorize requirements among groups and assign each a code.

It would be best to have a coding table that looks like Table 2, typically a spreadsheet. This will help in later stages in expanding the table with additional information.

#	Type	Subtype	User
R11	Functional	—	Jone
R12	Nonfunctional	Availability	Kevin

Table 2 Coding table

Competition Analysis (for New Software Only)

Building new, first-time software for a startup and crafting the requirements will be based on customer analysis. However, you need to identify one extra component: the competitive feature. Usually, the customer requests something that no other competitor covers in their current offerings. Because of this, you should create a needs matrix since not all needs are identical. Usually, a competition analysis precedes this step. But you can reverse engineer a competitor's needs statement to see what your new product or service covers versus that of the competition. Because the product ideally will have the edge over the competition, analyze what you can provide that your competitors lack. I have always found that a spider chart offers the best visualization in this case.

In the first step, collect public information about the competition and the offered features and compare it to what you already gathered from the users.

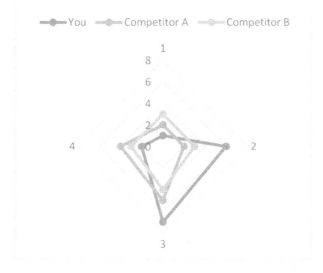

Figure 30 Competition analysis

In this comparison, divide requirements into four categories:

- **Primary need**: Without it, the product will not fulfill its function.
- **Secondary need**: These will support the primary need and make the product more desirable but will not add function.
- **Hidden need**: This is an issue unfulfilled by other products or services, and no one else in the market is providing it.
- **Importance needs**: These features will make the buying decision easier for the customer.

Following is an example of using a "smart timer" as a product to evaluate collected customer needs:

- The battery lasts for a long time (primary need)
- The controls are exact (primary need)
- The system has an auto-respond feature (hidden need)
- Easy to understand (secondary need)
- The system has a power-saving function (primary need)
- The system will be economical (importance need)

#	Type	Subtype	User	Need Type
R11	Functional	—	Jone	Primary
R12	Nonfunctional	Availability	Kevin	Primary

Table 3 Requirements categories

Expand the coding table with one column to consolidate all functions. Usually, final requirements are reduced to about a third of those listed in the coding table. This reduction occurs not because you have dropped requirements but because you translated the requirements, and many will be similar or a small extension of existing requirements.

Step 2: Translation of the Requirements

Translation of the requirements means converting the requirements' format and wording from one state to another. Remove each stakeholder's way of explaining the need from the actual need. This usually will occur if you follow five main guidelines for writing need statements:

- What, not how
- Specificity
- Positive, not negative
- Avoid *must* and *should*
- Avoid ambiguous words

The most critical guideline is what, not how. Most customers will tell you how to solve a problem, but you need to know the problem, not how they think a solution would solve it. If they provide a solution, that's great. Keep it. Some users are tech-savvy and might offer insights that will be helpful in the design.

When translating, one statement can generate multiple needs. Break these down as well. A user statement can be translated into a single requirement. Here's an example:

Statement: *"It took me one week to learn how to do it, so it had better be easy."*

Translation: "The product is easy to use."

Try to avoid ambiguous words such as those listed in Table 4.

Qualifiers	all, every, always, sometimes, only, often, none, never, usually
Comparatives	small as, bigger than, smaller than, like
Quantities	some, few, a lot of
Positional words	after, before
Temporal words	from, until, when
Joining words	and, or, both

Table 4 Ambiguous words

Once the requirements are coded and translated, the next phase is identifying conflicts.

Step 3: Conflict Analysis

The requirements document should specify the system's goals using statements such as "the system should" or "the system could." Identify what you mean by the word *system*. Is it the current or the to-be system? Is it only the software? Or the software and the environment in which it operates (the domain)?

For example, if a user is editing a specific item, can other users also edit this item? These questions may seem like basic common sense, but they need to be asked to simplify the process of software development.

The requirements need to be in a simple form, for example, (: Field state = typing if character count >0 within 3 seconds). Include assumptions and expectations. The user is finished typing if the field has no character added in the past three seconds. The field will unlock. Be sure to achieve this level of detail to ensure there are no assumptions during the development phase.

Based on the quantity of the requirements, you might build an interaction matrix to identify dependencies and conflicts, and which parts conflict with which other parts. But I find this is too much work and rarely used. Since most requirements will show no conflict, approach the conflict issue on a goal-by-goal basis or via a primary functional and nonfunctional requirements category. (Usually, each category will have 12 or so requirements.)

	R1	R2	R3	R4	Total
R1	N/A	0	0	1	1
R2	1	N/A	0	0	1
R3	1	0	N/A	1	2
R4	0	0	0	N/A	0

Table 5 Interaction matrix

A *goal* is the business problem the software is trying to solve, so another way of discovering conflicts is by categorizing requirements by goal types:

- **Soft goals** describe a state preferred among multiple alternative behaviors. These goals identify a specific state that is neither true nor false. An example: The system needs to be simple for users aged 40 to 60.
- **Hard goals** describe the software's specific behavior, like things to maintain or avoid and the desired result. Detail

hard goals using an "if" statement: for example, "If a special condition occurs, then do take or don't take a specific action."

Categorizing all your requirements under goals reduces potential conflict because it shows all statements related to one segment of work in one location, which will help in resolving requirement conflicts later. If a requirement conflicts with the primary goal of the application, it will be removed. If you do find conflicting requirements, you can take one of three steps:

- Go back to the requirement owner and explain why this element will be dropped.
- Look for a way around the conflict.
- Change one of the conflicting requirements with the stakeholder's approval.

Prioritizing Requirements

This is where priorities enter the mix and rearrange the requirements. Quantify the relative importance of each need. When prioritizing the requirements, two forces will decide the priority level:

- The commonality of the need
- Risk of the need

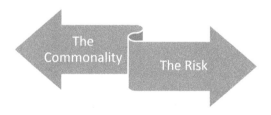

Figure 31 Commonality and risk

Commonality Analysis

The easiest way to prioritize needs is to examine how often users request them:

- Frequently requested (more than three times)
- Commonly requested (two or three times)

- Specific case (one time)

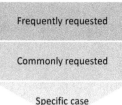

Figure 32 Commonality analysis

Once you translate all requirements into a statement, start to create the needs list. For the commonality analysis, create an importance column detailing the number of user requests for each item.

#	User Need	Need	Importance
1	The product is easy to use	R1, R11, R34, R35	4
2	The product cost is low	R23, R55, R56, R78, R33	5

Table 6 Commonality table

Decide relative priority for each need based on commonality. By focusing on the most common needs first, you help ensure that most users' needs are satisfied and produce a broader impact on the organization.

Risk Analysis

The risk in this context is not finishing the requirements and how to predict that. Here is a three-step process for conducting a risk analysis:

1. Learn the dependencies among requirements and create requirements groups.
2. Estimate the duration of the requirements.
3. Calculate the final need.

(You can add, as another factor, the development cost.)

The first step is fairly straightforward—expand the table and list all dependencies of this requirement, though you will need help from the SME in most cases. You typically do that by building a relationship matrix.

Relationship Matrix

As the name suggests, the relationship matrix is the relationship between two things: the use case and the requirements. It's used for tracking requirements mapping. It could also be used for the system/owner or service/system.

Let's take the use case as an example. You start by listing the use cases in the first column, then list all the requirements in the first row, and then mark the cells that map to this use case.

	REQ1	REQ2	REQ3	REQ4	REQ5	REQ6	REQ7	REQ8	REQ9	REQ10	REQ11	REQ12	REQ13	REQ14	REQ15	REQ16	REQ17
Use case 1	x			x				x			x						x
Use case 2			x				x				x		x		x	x	
Use case 3				x								x	x				
Use case 4		x						x				x					
Use case 5						x			x					x			
Use case 6	x		x								x		x		x	x	

Table 7 Relationship matrix

Duration Estimation

To estimate durations, you will create story points. User stories are summarized as points that include duration estimates from their respective developers. Combined, these provide an overview of the total story completion effort and time. When getting the three-point estimate, ask developers to estimate the likelihood of each point. That is, the best and worst cases and the scenario most likely to be achieved. This will involve a calculation of the average by scoring the best versus the worst: (Best +4* Most likely + Worst)/6)

This can also be expressed as the most probable time (TM+), optimistic time (TO), pessimistic time (TP), and exact time (TE).

Next, decide the velocity.

Velocity is the speed at which you finish the story points per sprint. The more the team finishes, the higher the velocity. Measure story points after a few sprints for an insight into team productivity standards. This will help in estimating future work.

If you encounter something that cannot be estimated, or the estimation is quite high, you can "timebox" it. In other words, you can designate time to work on it regardless of the results. Once that is done, you will face two possible scenarios:

1. You will have an accurate duration estimate midway through the story development.
2. Time will run out, and there will be no available estimate. In this case, the pursuit may be considered a poor requirement or one needing further clarification. (This outcome is rare.)

The previous two points illustrate the concept of the cone of uncertainty: the closer you are to project completion, the more accurate your estimates are. Experience helps reduce variations, but the shape of the cone is the same.

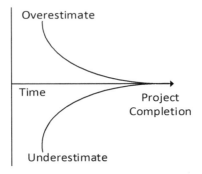

Figure 33 *The cone of uncertainty*

Over time, you should be able to compare the proposed timetable to the newly projected estimates. At this point, it may be helpful to ask developers to update their duration estimations.

Prioritization Calculation

By now, you have created the dependencies and durations and identified priorities, as well as additional information.

Requirements	Dependency	Assigned group	Contribution to the goal	Cost of development	Duration	Priority
Goal 1						
Requirement 1	—	G1	4	100	2 W	1
Requirement 2	R1	G1	2	200	3 W	2
Requirement 3	—	G2	2	70	1 W	1
Requirement 4	R2	G1	1	20	3 D	3
Requirement 5	—	G3	1	90	2 W	1
Requirement 6	R1	G1	3	160	5 W	2

Table 8 Prioritization calculation

In the contribution to the goal column, identify how core each requirement relates to the goal. For example, a log-on screen is a requirement; but achieving value hinges on users' ability to log in.

In this step, rank values from 1 to 4, where 1 contributes little to the added value, and 4 contributes significantly. The ranges are flexible, based on the needs. But you must follow the same ranking criteria for all requirements comparisons, whatever numbering system you choose. But I usually do the following:

*The order = (Priority * Contribution) / (Duration + Dependency count)*

The higher the ranking, the more critical the requirement is to the project. To make this formula work:

- *Duration* is a fixed unit for all evaluations. It encompasses, for example, hours, days, and weeks.
- *Dependency count* is how many other dependencies have to finish before developing it.

Start by using the formula for requirements with the highest priority and contribution levels, relatively low duration of development, and the fewest dependencies. Then begin testing more difficult requirements, those with higher dependencies, and so on.

Please note that all the mentioned requirements are intended to develop the MVP. (They are all core.) This will help you plan the sprints with the project manager.

Analyzing Requirements

Requirements should be complete, clear, consistent with the other requirements, and include measurable data so you can write the needs in a meaningful way. A good way to validate the requirements is to perform a requiments swap. In other words, validate requirements with different tiers of users to ensure they are unambiguous. The first step in analyzing requirements is to draw the necessary diagrams for software implementation. This way, you will see how elements integrate and relate. Many diagrams can help in this effort. The most popular in Agile is the use case diagram.

Use Case Diagram

The use case diagram is a high-level description of the requirements. Each use case is a stand-alone activity. It includes the agents and the system interaction necessary to generate a result. Use cases are bigger than user stories in Agile but smaller than in epic. Therefore, group the stories (requirements) into use cases. Each use case needs the following:

- Meta (date created, update, by who, case name, and so on)
- Actor (the agent)
- Description
- Pre-condition (before the request)
- Post-condition (the output from the request)
- The steps from the pre-condition to the post-condition
- Any business rules
- Any assumptions

For each pre-condition and step, you can create a negative scenario that examines the effect of users who do the unexpected. This step evaluation can be useful, especially in security. To avoid conflict, always create a definition and abbreviation table (glossary) for readers that shows your intent. This is one way to reduce conflict due to misunderstanding. Use clear, simple language.

In use case diagrams, the stories will connect. There are two types of connections:

- **Extended connection** is used under specific conditions. Usually, its purpose is to add specialized functionality to a base use case (like a prerequisite checker or registration form).
- **"Include use case"** (sometimes called a use-use case). The base use case triggers it under all conditions. Its purpose is to simplify the base use case, make it smaller, and allow a specific function across multiple use cases.

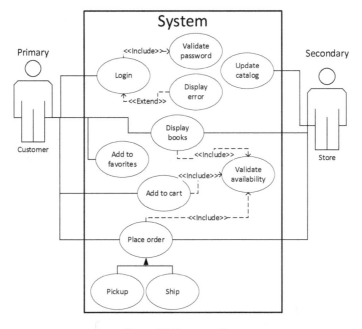

Figure 34 Use case diagram

This is the use case for a system. The bold frame represents the system boundaries.

Create Systems Test Cases

At this stage, you should be very certain of what will be developed, and thinking about how you will test it. Test-driven development (writing the test before writing the code) is gaining traction nowadays. For the first wave of tests, choose requirements with no dependencies. These should be the easiest to conduct. You might divide the first wave (priority 1) into multiple phases. After the first round, begin tests based on the dependency chain.

First, let's discuss what is meant by the *test*. There are many tests available:

- **Integration testing**: This tests groups of subsystems (collection of subsystems) and eventually an entire system, and the developer typically conducts it.
- **System testing**: This tests the entire system. The developer typically does it.
- **UI (end-to-end testing)**:
  - The developer does the test.
  - This tests how the end user will use the application.
- **Security testing**:
  - Developers do this.
  - This looks for flows in the code to prevent data leakage in production.
  - There are two kinds of security testing
    - **Dynamic testing** tests a specific attack type and executes a battery of attacks to test the system. The downside is that it requires the full system to run; it takes a long time.
    - **Static testing** scans the code (in the non-running state) and highlights possible vulnerabilities.
- **Performance testing** encompasses many tests, including sock, spike, and step tests.
- **Acceptance testing** evaluates system adoption by the client/end user. Testing involves typical transactions.

Usually, each story needs multiple tests to test the product's functionality, although the most critical of all is the user acceptance testing.

How to Write Test Cases for User Acceptance Testing

To write test cases, start with one requirement or group of requirements. Follow a step-by-step guide, including any deviations. It's common practice to group multiple requirements for testing in the same scenario. For example:

Test Group A

1. Log in to the OS.
2. Go to www.web-software-example.com.
3. Set the username to Jim.
4. Use the password 123.
5. Press enter.

This will impact test cases 1A, 2B, and 3C.

- Success, the system logs you in.
- Failure, the system does not log you in or gives an error.

When login succeeds:

1. Go to the upper left corner.
2. Select new customer.
3. A new page will open to record customer information.
4. Enter the following.
5. Customer Name: Tom.
6. Customer phone 12345667.
7. Customer address 12, NY.
8. Comments: This is a test for the comments.
9. Press Save and close.

(Test cases 54, ii56)

- Success, the system saves and accepts the new customer.
- Failure, the system shows an error, or the form doesn't work.

If this step succeeds:

1. Go to the upper right corner.
2. Press show customer.
3. The newly entered customer name should appear.

(Test cases 876 2te c56)

- Success, the user appears in the users list.
- Failure, the user doesn't appear in the list.

Collecting Feedback

If you ask people what they want, you might miss important opportunities. Try to observe them as well. A problem might be unnoticeable to the user. Create a list of feedback based on user comments and observations. When all feedback is collected, rank the findings by priority:

- 0—Not a usability problem
- 1—Cosmetic problem
- 2—Minor usability problem
- 3—Major usability problem, important to fix
- 4—Usability catastrophe, imperative to fix

Never ask for immediate feedback. You will get either a user who will provide only minimum feedback or an overly enthusiastic user who will share lots of unnecessary comments. Instead, a structured feedback process dramatically improves outcomes. No one user must be allowed to retest the same function. All functions should be tested only one time by different users to ensure that you are collecting the initial reactions. It's also possible to collect feedback during the test.

Build Product Road Map

The product road map is the product manager's responsibility, or the product leader's, but sometimes you might be asked to provide one based on the features requested. A road map defines the key features and characteristics of the product in the upcoming releases. It's used to plan and prioritize features for delivering the product. It usually looks like a table

MVP	Year1–Q1	Q2	Q3	Q4
Feature 1	Feature 5	Feature 9	Feature 6	Feature 4
Feature 2	Feature 3		Feature 8	
			Feature 11	

Table 9 Product road map

The idea is to place and plan which feature to go in which quarter. This planning happens before sprint planning or even reaching the backlog stage. All of this is from the product's overall vision. You could utilize the *purpose alignment model* created by Niel

Nickolaisen. It's a prioritization model for prioritizing features or any business-related objective. In this model, you rank features based on two axes:

- **Market differentiation**: these are the things that drive value to our customers
- **Mission critical**: these are the things critical to the operations.

These two parameters will lead every feature to be in one of four quadrants:

- **Partner**: these are the features that we should partner with someone else to deliver.
- **Differentiating**: these are the features that are critical to operations and help us gain market share.
- **Parity** is the feature we must provide to maintain a minimum market.
- **Who cares?** These features are neither market differentiating nor mission critical.

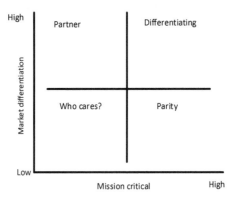

Figure 35 *Purpose alignment model*

When you develop a product, there will always be this one big customer who wants this specific feature that no one else wants. Usually, Sales will push to include it in the next release. But doing so could derail the product from the remaining customers. The rule of thumb is that if what this big customer is requesting is simple or a feature that is already on the road map, you accept this change; otherwise, stick to the road map.

If the product lacks market information, as with an internal product for the organization's use, categorize the features into three main groups:

- o Functional
- o Nonfunctional
- o UI/UX

You start with the functional ones, working your way to the nonfunctional ones while maintaining constant minimum interface changes.

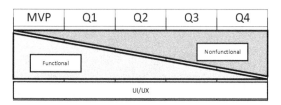

Figure 36 Features and road map

The Requirements Document

Sometimes, you might need this document as one of the project milestones, or the customer is requesting it to be delivered as one of the project deliverables. The requirements document includes the following sections:

- Introduction (purpose of the document, product scope, glossary terms, requirement sources, general overview, the system as-is, and the system to-be)
- Description (product perspective)
- Functions of the new software
- Assumptions (about users, domain, and the environment)
- Specific requirements (all the tables and diagrams mentioned previously)

Numbering should follow a specific hierarchy. For example, goal 1, requirement 1 should be G1R1. This system makes tracing easy. Never go beyond three levels. (R1 is one level, R1.1 is two levels, and R1.1.1 is three levels—the maximum.) If you need more, then divide that group in half.

The requirements document is purely Waterfall. It's a massive document explaining everything about the software requirements. See the online "IEEE Std 830 standards template" for an example. The template is old but might give you some ideas.

Chapter 5: Project Execution Approach (Agile Approach)

....

At this point in the project, if you follow the sequence of this book, you should:

- Have an approved system proposal
- Have a requirements document for at least 5% of the overall system requirements.

The next step is deciding on the project execution approach—Agile or Waterfall. So, let's start with an Agile understanding to ensure a good grasp of the subject. But first, let's agree on a few things:

o Agile is not a *tool*.
o Agile is not coding first and building the documentation and design later.
o *Agile should provide quick business value.*
o Agile is not a multiphased project.
o Agile is not *chaos*.
o Agile is not a method dictated by someone, a group, or an organization.
o Agile is not a ragged process. It's about making sense to deliver value.

If you feel the team is suffering from any of these points, that would be because the team has "fake Agile." The previous points are only a few signs that this is fake Agile. Although, as you might have noticed in the above list, the statement "Agile should provide quick business value" is the essential Agile aspect that trumps any other problem.

When we say the word *agile*, do we mean Agile project management, *Agile Manifesto*, or the word *agile* itself? The more accurate response is a mix of all of these. We use this term when the team can respond quickly to changes and deliver results as the business demands. Business demands are not customers changing their minds about requirements that have already been collected and developed. This is a standard scope change in such a case, also called a *change request*.

Agile methodology collects requirements in phases and executes them in phases, allowing the business to adjust the project's direction as the *political, economic, social, technological, environmental*, and *legal* factors (PESTEL.) situation develops.

A full spectrum of methods is available to cover this definition. This chapter's purpose is to introduce you to the concepts of the Agile mindset. But to simplify things a bit, there are two main methods to deliver and control the value to the business. In other words, Agile ways.

The spiral: A project starts with the fewest possible options; then, the team adds options and features until the team reaches the desired goal. The team adds features and enhancements by employing small changes.

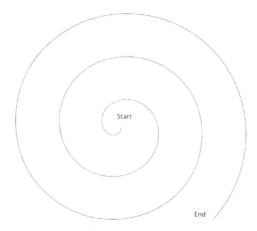

Start

End

Figure 37 Spiral

Flow smoothing: This enables more consistent flow from start to finish and alleviates the bottlenecks. Applying flow control and process enhancement will lead to much more volume in the end.

Make the flow consistent by adjusting the pipeline away from random sizes leading to many queues. Implementing flow control results in uniform size, which leads to a more consistent flow of tasks and activities.

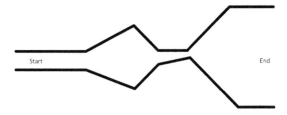

Figure 38 *Flow pipeline*

Usually, the team starts with the spiral process and then makes the pipeline of tasks (in the spiral) work smoothly. This is usually done case by case. In some cases, the team suffers from task imbalance, is overloaded in some steps, and has only a few tasks in other actions; having this type of imbalance might allow flow control methods to solve many issues. In such cases, implement flow smoothing first.

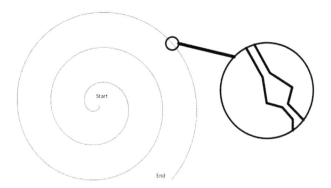

Figure 39 *Relation between the spiral and the pipeline*

The good news is that you can apply both methods. You could use one spiral method and one flow smoothing method for maximum efficiency, but this is usually quite difficult. Using just one will improve the delivered results regardless of whether you apply the spiral or the flow smoothing method.

Many Agile methods are already growing to the point that they have some of each (spiral and flow smoothing). Some incorporate so many techniques that it's more expensive and delivers slower results than Waterfall. Unfortunately, sometimes we love one methodology over another, thinking this is the best option available.

In reality, there is no Golden Rule. The answer is always based on the situation. This is why you need to understand each method's pros and cons to select the best option to deliver value to the business. Agile methodologies are many. Here are a few:

- Extreme programming (spiral)
- Scrum (spiral + flow smoothing)
- Lean software development (flow smoothing)
- Kanban (flow smoothing)
- Value stream mapping (flow smoothing)

Though each method has many books written on it that provide more details, I have collected the following key takeaways from each.

Extreme Programming

Extreme programming (XP) takes the everyday aspects of programming and focuses on improving aspects like communication, simplicity, feedback, respect, and courage. In XP, all the team roles are on one level, with releases as small as possible and as frequent as possible.

Extreme Programming Practices

Extreme programming has 12 practices (rules). In XP, the implementation is all or none. You cannot implement it partially. You must apply the 12 practices, or the team will not achieve results:

1. **The game planning**: The customer and the developers plan the products. The client and the developer develop a list of new features for them. Each feature is presented as a user story, the development team estimates the effort of each story, and the clients and the development team prioritize the stories.
2. **Small releases**: Plan the releases to be as small as possible and as frequent as possible.
3. **System metaphor**: Use metaphors that are easy to understand and even nontechnical.
4. **Simple design**: Make the designs as simple as they can be.

5. **Continuous testing**: Write the test before the code. The idea is to use the test as an executable form of administering the requirements (test-driven development).
6. **Refactoring**: Improve the design of the code to allow new features to be added easily.
7. **Pair programming**: Two developers will pair (work side by side) on one code at one workstation. This is extreme in code review, but the benefits from the quality improvement will reduce waste in troubleshooting and code review.
8. **Collective code ownership**: Anyone can add to any part of the code. Success and failure are attributed to the team, not to individuals.
9. **Continuous integrations**: Sometimes, the individual parts of the code easily pass unit testing, but when all the parts are put together, issues start to appear. This practice calls for integrating code continuously or as often as possible. The XP recommendation is to do it daily.
10. **Forty-hour work week**: This avoids overburn of resources. XP allows only 40 hours of work per week. You can add one additional total of 40 hours per project. Anything more than that signals something wrong in the project timeline and management.
11. **On-site customer**: One customer representative as a single point of contact should be available to answer any question during the development.
12. **Coding standard**: Apply the same code formatting and coding convention across all teams.

Some other practices for XP:

- Require people to be able to work on any workstation.
- No dedication of any resources, including things such as open workspace. Everyone should be able to use any of the resources.
- All development team members should face one another and not the walls.
- A whiteboard or flip chart must always be available to explain ideas as needed.

XP Top Issues

- **It's an all-or-nothing approach**: You cannot adopt some parts of the XP model and expect XP results. It is all or nothing.
- **Unrealistic expectations**: It may be unrealistic to expect the client to be available during the entire duration of the development, or to have only one representative who knows all the answers.

Scrum

Another widespread agile method is Scrum. It's the most common methodology worldwide and the most often thought of when we say, "Agile project management." But a word of caution—if not executed properly and not customized based on the environment, it will lead to poorer results than other methods. Scrum has lots of books written on every aspect of it. In other words, it's still evolving. Here is a quick overview of Scrum terminology:

- **Sprints** are the loops that the project goes into to produce value. The shorter, the better. The typical sprint duration is two weeks, with a maximum of four weeks. Adjust these values to fit project needs.

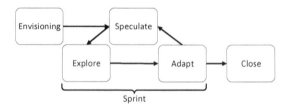

Figure 40 Agile project phases

- **The backlog** is a list of what the team will deliver; it is a view of all the items in the queue.

Sprint Phases

- **Envisioning phase**: Determining what the project is trying to build, chartering the project, and building the team.
- **Speculate phase**: The first sprint phase, deciding what features (requirements to satisfy business needs) you will include in the sprint. The feature-based delivery plan

estimates risks. Maintain a feature board showing the progress and issue logs of the sprint and the overall project.

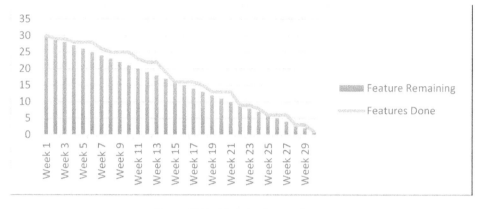

Figure 41 Backlog chart example

- **Explore phase**: The second phase of the sprint. This includes actual planned work, a review of developed features, and build issue management. Once finished, the team prioritizes the features built and the task estimates.
- **Adapt phase**: The third and final phase of the sprint. Issues are fixed, a review is finalized, and lessons are learned. The project will loop until all sprints are finished. Collect feedback.
- **Close phase**: Deliverables are completed and help produce the lessons learned from the project.

Scrum Pillars

Scrum is based on three pillars:
- **Transparency**: Everyone can see every part of the project.
- **Inspection**: Inspect work products to detect any deviations.
- **Adaptation**: The team will adapt and make corrections if deviations are detected.

Scrum Events

Events are distinctive to the methodology. The four primary Scrum events are:

- **Sprint planning**: Sprints are one to four weeks long. At the end of a sprint, some business value will be delivered. Sprint planning occurs at the beginning to determine what will be done in the sprint.
- **Daily Scrum**: This quick meeting happens daily to discuss ongoing tasks and what is needed to accomplish them.
- **Sprint review**: This happens at the end of the sprint to review whether the sprint achieved the goals.
- **Sprint retrospective**: After the sprint review, adjust the backlog with the product owner based on the sprint lessons learned.

Scrum Roles

Scrum has roles (unlike XP's flat structure). They are:

- Scrum master
- Product owner
- Development team

Scrum Master

The orchestrator of the entire scrum process, the Scrum master works with the product owners and the development team. Their responsibilities to the product owners are to:

- Find techniques to manage the backlog
- Ensure the product owners prioritize the backlog to get the maximum value

Their responsibilities within the development team are:

- Coaching the team to self-organize
- Removing development roadblocks
- Facilitating Scrum events

Scrum master is the counterpart of the project manager in Waterfall, both on the same level in a project.

Product Owner

The product owner is responsible for making decisions about the product. The owner decides what will be built by prioritizing the backlog of features. The product owner in Scrum is similar to a business analyst, although the primary focus of the product owner is the product, and they represent the voice of the customer.

This role is entirely different from the product owner in marketing. The marketing role is all about one product and how to get it sold. They do that by prioritizing features and the overall likability of the product. Both roles have basically the same name—product owner/product manager—but this distinction is vital if you plan to add more modules from the IT-TNG framework.

Development Team

The team is self-organizing. Members decide how to build working software/features based on the product owner's input. Also, the team takes turns in quality review and coding. Usually, the team has around seven developers plus or minus three (not including the Scrum master and the product owner).

The definition of "done" is critical in a scrum, and all teams must agree on it initially. Usually, the feature is done when it's coded, tested, and documented. In the *Agile Manifesto*, progress must be tracked by the done features.

Lean Software Development

Lean is agile. A lot of Agile methodologies are based on lean. Lean development is a way of analyzing both principles and ideas and providing some tools. Some Agile concepts come from this way of thinking. The most common principles are:

- **Eliminating waste**: In lean, anything is considered waste if it's not adding value. So, if it did not add value, it would be removed from the development process.
- **Amplifying learning**: Explore the idea and gain knowledge before taking action. If you fail, you will learn quickly.
- **Defer commitment**: Instead of taking the first yes or the first acceptance from the customer and running with it, consider offering alternative options and learn what is most appealing. Then decide on the path to follow.

- **Deliver as quickly as possible**: Develop the option for the customer as quickly as possible so you can choose your path. Once you have decided, push for it as quickly as possible.
- **Empower the team**: Let developers do what they do best, empowering them to deliver the expected value. Trust them to do so.
- **Build quality**: In writing code to solve a problem, you write the code to pass the test. Pair programming can advance quality. So can good documentation, efficient code, and commenting on the code.
- **See the whole**: The whole must be coherent. This includes attention to how each piece of the puzzle fits. This ability is crucial to delivering value.

Kanban

Kanban's primary concept is limiting the work in progress (WIP) by allowing only a specific number of activities to run within a unit. The amount of WIP will be based on the unit capacity. This avoids cluttering the unit with too many activities that can dilute its focus. Instead, the focus can be on a specific set of activities.

Cycle time in kanban is how long one piece of work takes from entering the first column to exiting all the steps. The objective is to reduce the average cycle time and optimize to achieve the reduction.

Kanban is a process tool. Usually, it's done using a project board with tasks written on sticky notes from beginning to end. This simple method is suitable, especially in small teams. It will be inefficient to use a complex methodology if you have a small group. Kanban solves this because it is a lightweight method and can be described as a tool that integrates with other methodologies to improve efficiency. There are four main rules to applying kanban:

1. **Visualize your steps**: Place them into columns. Each column should have subcolumns with "doing" and "done" designations. The done subcolumn can be an activities buffer for the next step in the process.

2. **Limit the work in progress**: There is a specific number of tasks that can be performed in a particular step.
3. **Manage the flow**: Always ensure the tasks are moving from beginning to end, and if a bottleneck shows up, try to optimize it.
4. **Make policies explicit**: An example is defining the meaning of "done."

Applying these four rules over and over will allow you to optimize the process further, so start from the current process. After a few iterations, you will discover the improvement kanban promises.

Backlog	Analysis (2)		Development (2)		Testing (1)	Released (1)	Deployed (1)
	Ongoing	Done	Ongoing	Done			
A	X						
B		X					
C				X			
D						X	
E					X		

Table 10 Kanban

*The numbers in parentheses are to limit the WIP.

Value Stream Mapping

Map the activities of the process to analyze any issue. Value stream mapping is from the world of process improvement. The philosophy behind it is to identify value-added work (the value to the end customer or the end service or product).

Identifying such value will allow you to calculate each task's efficiency (how many minutes you spend on a task contributing to the end product). The first step is to identify the need for optimization. Even if it is an inefficient process, it will still deliver the needed results and allow the elimination of waste.

Value stream mapping comes after easier practices like kanban. Building value stream maps requires a few measurements in order to draw the existing system:

- **Identify** the major process activities.
- **Count** the employees (resources) and calculate the percentage of their time dedicated to a task.

- **Project and envision** processing time for this activity (the average resource's time consumed to finish the task).
- **Measure utilization**, the percentage of activities done during the time designated.

Agile at Scale

Typically, Agile teams comprise fewer than 10 people, but what if you have 10 teams? Each team has 10 people. In this case, you take one team out of the 10 teams. Dedicate nine teams to product development, and the one remaining team will have the following functions:

1. Architect the solution, dividing the final product into major subparts and leaving it to individual teams to decide how to deal with it.
2. Lay down standards for work (what will be used and what will not be used at a very high level).
3. Defining the outcome desired from each team (technically).
4. Identify the integration between the components.
5. Maintain product backlog for the entire product.
6. Prioritize some elements in team sprints to allow faster production of MVP.
7. Rotation. This to share experience and build bridges between different teams. You need to move one team member from each team to another team if they are free. Each team member will be moved once. It's best to use a lottery system to avoid team morale impact during project initiation.

Parts of the product will be simpler than others. This is where *swarming* comes in. Whoever finishes first will rush to validate (QA) the others' work. In some cases, one or more teams will have difficulty completing their part, so in this case, some of the backlogs for these teams will be shifted to other teams.

The final step in Agile at scale is paying the technical debt. Each team usually has a slight variation in how they do things. This variation will make the final product compatible but not flow right. So, sometimes, the governing team needs to perform code refactoring for some part to make the entire code concise. Usually, this issue disappears after a few projects and the do's and don'ts have been defined.

If you notice, Agile at scale is almost the same concept as running projects inside a program.

If you are interested in this, you can read a pretty good deployment of Agile at scale on Spotify. They divided the team into tribes, squads, chapters, and guilds. I'm not too fond of a company adopting another company's model since each has its own challenges. I would always prefer for a company to develop its own model. But learning the patterns and studying what others have tried to do can help expedite the process.

)

Chapter 6: Finding the Best Mix for the Best Business Value

••••••••••••••••••••••••••••••

This is the challenging part. The term *agile* differs from the term Agile methodology or Agile software development. Sometimes, it's more agile to use the Waterfall model. The agility to adapt to changing requirements is different from the Agile methodology. But tweak these approaches to meet the needs. For example, the software development cycle has four main phases. Each can be a blend of Agile and Waterfall. It's all on one spectrum. In other words, you may start the project employing Waterfall but conduct quality testing via Agile.

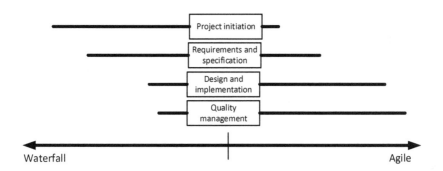

Figure 42 Agile and Waterfall mix

This will lead to what forms you can choose from to deliver each part of the project. But first, let's get an overview of the building blocks.

Possible Forms of Value Delivery

So, with this in mind, we can extrapolate three possible states:

- Agile
- Waterfall
- Somewhere in between

Agile

In this format, you don't have a full vision from the customer, so the project starts with MVP (minimum viable product) and builds around it. With this approach, prototypes can play a critical role. This is usually the case when developing a new product and in almost all start-ups.

In Figure 43, each circle represents a requirement gathering phase, and each square is an application release. In some application releases, there may be no need to collect requirements. Two or three times through the spiral should suffice. Gathering requirements will be based on whether your progress aligns with the customer's vision.

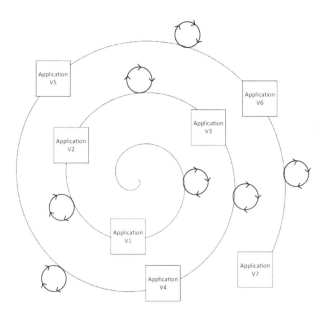

Figure 43 Requirements in Agile native

The spiral diagram shows how a complex application can be effectively broken into chunks and progress to full-fledged software.

Waterfall

Waterfall calls for one massive requirement gathering phase leading to the development of the first application. You can usually make several change requests afterward to adjust the software. In rare cases, you might have one or two adjustments to the course midway. But this usually occurs only in long projects.

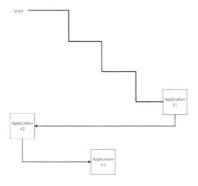

Figure 44 *Requirements in Waterfall*

Somewhere in Between

Some try to mix both worlds by merging the big requirement gathering at the beginning and frequent releases as soon as a feature is ready. Though this is not 100 percent Agile, it delivers faster value to the business and is well accepted in the industry as Agile.

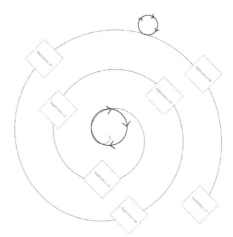

Figure 45 *Requirements for Waterfall and Agile delivery*

In other words, do the requirements gathering and the design using Waterfall build the initial understanding. Then do a Waterfall project to fulfill these requirements and release it to the customer, usually through a multiphase Waterfall. Once MVP is finished, switch to Agile.

Note: You could still use the CI/CD and Agile tools in Waterfall. The only difference is in the definition of "done."

Build the Road Map to Optimize Value

From previous diagrams (Agile and Waterfall), it's evident that Agile requires more work and that Waterfall is much easier. But the time it takes to generate version 1 in Waterfall is much longer, and the ability to respond to changes is limited. Another positive impact of Waterfall for a small project or application is that it's much quicker to execute in one shot.

Agile is useful when there are uncertainties in a project. These can involve uncertainty in the requirements, market conditions, or another experiment with some unknown factor. In such a situation, only build on what is known and adjust. But if the project doesn't have any of those variables or, conversely, it has acceptable risk limits, it's better to do it all in one shot (or multiphased Waterfall). Otherwise, it is wasting resources on Agile while the scope is predetermined. So, generally, you make the selection base on two criteria:

- The economics of a methodology
- The velocity requirements

Economics of the Methodology

When selecting one module over another, base the choice on the project and the customer's requirements. Many factors enter into choosing a methodology for the software project journey. It is challenging to select the best method that meets the project objective and analyze the costs and benefits. Using advanced tactics like XP and Scrum to implement every software project is possible. But remember that the waste will be significant in some projects.

So, before committing to a method, consider these three main factors:

- Frequency of changes (customers change their minds, or you need to shift gears to take different directions).
- Level of certainty in requirements (requirement risk).
- Cost of governance.

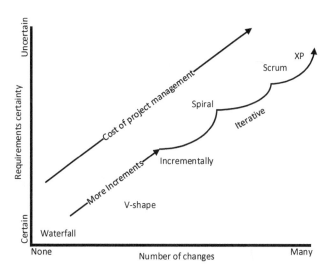

Figure 46 Economics of Agile

Combining the three factors will place your project in one or more locations in the diagram.

There may be a few anticipated changes and almost certain requirements. In this case, Waterfall will be best. But building new software to seize new market opportunities requires being quite agile. If it's not possible to anticipate how many changes are needed, or even the certainty of the requirements, the project will go into loops of collect, build, test, and adjust, then repeat. During the iterative phase, you may add increments to build the product and rebuild the entire product over and over to drive more value.

The third issue is the cost of governance. This is the project management practice cost. Each situation will direct you to a specific methodology since there is no best or one-size-fits-all methodology.

For example, if you have a very limited project management budget, go with Waterfall and consider dividing it into smaller projects to reduce risk. Since it is a Waterfall project, you might tweak it to a V-shape model. The V-shape model extends the Waterfall but runs multiple project phases simultaneously.

If you don't have the budget and insist on applying Scrum, you will have something that looks like a Scrum but operates as Waterfall. Unfortunately, this scenario becomes the case in lots of organizations and teams. This applies not only to project management costs but also to incremental costs. Each increment will require that additional valuable resources be allocated to testing and integration. The more increments, the more costly the project will become. If you go with a spiral type, costs will be even higher if you create throwaway prototypes that are later abandoned.

It all comes down to cost versus value and selecting which best-targeted value pairs with the acceptable cost. Deciding on a break-even point will help guide you to the correct methodology. Which one to apply is based on how much you can spend. Agile is not cheap. From observation, it's 1.5 times more expensive than Waterfall. In other words, if the project budget is 1M in Waterfall, you will need 1.5M to deliver it using Agile methods. What makes Agile attractive is the business's faster ROI, leading to more business benefits and generating revenue faster.

It's crucial to plan the business benefits against the project overall. For example, the business requires agility for only part of the project during the MVP phase and the first three months after launch. So, it makes sense to start Agile to deliver the required benefits faster and switch to Waterfall for a cheaper approach, or vice versa.

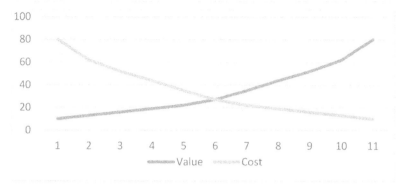

Figure 47 Cost versus value

Other factors can affect methodology choice. You might be unable to go to the extreme with the prototyping. Or you might jump between options, like building the minimum viable product as a Waterfall project and switching to a spiral later, depending on the circumstances.

True agility means deciding when to use a particular method based on the environment and each circumstance.

The Speed and the Deliverables

Velocity is the speed at which the team completes the required features. In Agile, velocity measures the team's capacity to execute the tasks utilizing story points, which means it's a relatively fixed ability. However, in Waterfall, the velocity has a compounded effect, allowing the project to finish more quickly. Of course, the delivered business value during the project is much less than with Agile, but the longer the project, the more quickly the results accumulate at the end. This would mean that Waterfall is not without benefits for the software project.

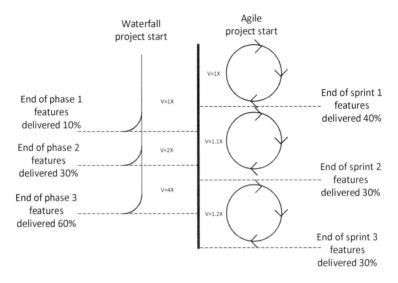

Figure 48 Velocity

Remember, it's all about what drives value to the organization more quickly. We sometimes assume that the organization wants the value in chunks, but sometimes they want it in full.

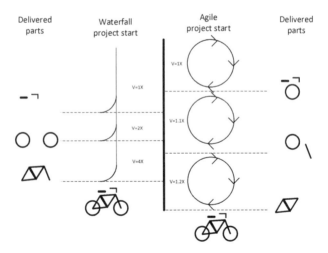

Figure 49 Value in chunks

This is why you choose your methodology case by case. In Figure 49, Agile will hurt the organization more than Waterfall. So, always validate this point to avoid wasting resources. The other way is utilizing throwaway prototypes. But in this case, the project delivers solutions to business problems, not iterative and accumulative build.

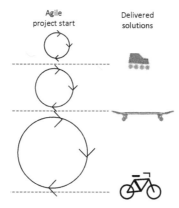

Figure 50 *Throwaway solutions*

Chapter 7: Project Execution

....

Now, you might be thinking, if I do all previous steps, I will have a pure Waterfall project with no Agile. This is partially true. Circling back to the beginning of the book, building the requirement document happens over time. It's not a one and done process, like in Waterfall.

This is the MVP—the minimum viable product. It is the simplest form of application. Build the requirement document around it and then go through the requirements gathering again. Create another version and repeat. If you decide to do requirements gathering as Waterfall and then perform the releases as Agile, that's also OK.

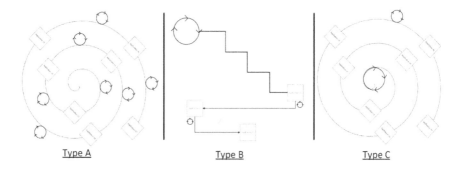

Type A   Type B   Type C

Figure 51 Project types

Both Types B and C require performing requirements gathering steps in full. If you are going for Type A, then the steps should be very lightweight. The entire process usually takes two weeks to run the lightweight version and three to four months if you are doing the full analysis.

Project Journey

The project journey is the project manager's primary responsibility, or the Scrum master's. Figure 52 shows how things should fit together.

The expected duration for each step is an estimate. It's based on experience level and the work to be done. But, in general, these numbers are expected averages and can be used as guides.

The project will be a seven-phase journey:

1. Chartering and teambuilding
2. Discover users' needs (user stories)
3. Develop high-level architecture
4. Release planning
5. Deliver, build, learn, and improve
6. UAT and training
7. Deploy to production

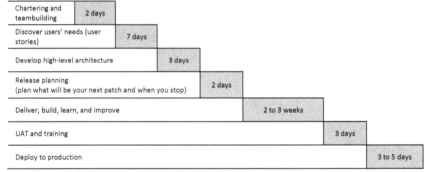

Figure 52 Agile project journey

Let's examine each of the phases.

Phase One: Chartering and Teambuilding

The first phase in the agile project is building the team and creating the project charter.

Project charter: This is the project description and who will benefit from it, usually a few pages summarizing the system proposal.

Team building: A *team* is a unit of two or more people communicating and coordinating members' work to reach a specific goal.

Types of Teams

- **Formal**, created by the organization to fulfill a need
- **Vertical**, manager and subordinates
- **Horizontal**, across departments (sometimes called the *project team*)

Team types can also be:

- **Local**, with members in the same location.
- **Virtual**, requiring a technology medium to facilitate communication.
- **Global**, from different parts of the world. The challenge is bridging time, distance, culture, and language.

	Formal	Vertical	Horizontal
Local team	Team 1		Team 4
Virtual team		Team 2	
Global team	Team 5		

Table 11 Team types

How to Decide on Team Size

The team needs to be large enough to incorporate multiple skill sets to benefit the project. At the same time, it needs to be small enough to make members feel connected.

Try to diversify. Heterogeneous teams perform better than homogeneous ones, although the former may have more conflict. Smaller teams perform faster. However, the exact number to achieve maximum success is based on many factors. Generally, three to six members is the golden range. If more members are needed, create multiple teams with objectives.

Building a team is the role of the team leader and the project manager. The team should have the following roles:

- Scrum master (usually this is the project manager)
- Product owner (business analyst)
- Developers

On larger projects, the backlog is divided between teams. Many existing setups have frameworks for that. A scaled agile framework (SAFe) is an example of this.

Phase Two: Discover Users' Needs (User Stories)

Here's a mock schedule to ensure you have the full picture. This example divides each working day into four slots, each two hours long. The working day is eight hours:

1. **Day 1**: Understand the business need and the required value.
2. **Day 2**: Understand the current system and what will be required.
3. **Day 3**: Define the stakeholders and send emails to them. Prepare the first round of questions.
4. **Day 4**: Conduct the first workshop to explain the application and collect ideas. Based on those, start planning the initial story maps and, most importantly, the activities.
5. **Day 5**: Present story maps, take core activities from the application, and start to compile more requirements as needed. These activities will represent one scenario. Advise stakeholders that there will be more sessions focused on additional scenarios. Conduct one-on-one interviews to collect additional requirements for the first scenario. Build initial user stories.
6. **Day 6**: Perform story building and activities to gather, prioritize, and analyze requirements. Since this involves only one scenario, it should be easy to accomplish in one day.
7. **Day 7**: Build both the use case diagrams and the test cases.

	Slot 1	Slot2	Slot 3	Slot 4
Day1	Identify needs		Sponsor and project manager interview	Document the day's findings
Day2	Content study phases one and two			Document the day's findings
Day3	Define your stakeholders		Plan your workshop and interview questions	
Day4	Brainstorming workshop 1		Build the initial story mapping	Buffer
Day5	Workshop 2: explore potential solutions and vote	Conduct one-on-one interviews		
Day6	Build stories	Requirements gathering activities	Prioritize requirements activities	Analyze requirements activities
Day 7	Build the use cases	Build test cases	Buffer	

Figure 53 BA schedule

At this point, you can either go back to the user for validation or start development. I find it unnecessary to validate at this stage since the information gathered so far is relatively limited. I typically move to the next phase.

Phase Three: Develop High-level Architecture

Usually, the design process of any IT-related system is divided into three main stages:

- **Requirement document**: This is the fundamental software requirement or the MVP requirements, at a minimum.
- **High-level design**: In the high-level design (HLD), highlight the customer's requirements and create an example to validate that you have the desired approach. This usually involves collaboration with architects.
- **Low-level design**: The low-level design (LLD) is more detailed. It has all the information about building the software, including the languages (not the source code), how things integrate, and so on. This is crafted among all team members from BA, architects, UI/UX, software development, and so on.

In some cases, both HLD and LLD are merged into one document, especially if the project is well known.

In some cases, you don't do the design at the start. You jump straight to coding from requirements. This is more common for small teams, small projects, or when there is time sensitivity. In those cases, designs are made at the end. These are called *as-built* designs.

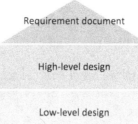

Requirement document

High-level design

Low-level design

Figure 54 Design levels

This pyramid will represent the details in each phase. Start with the requirements document and add the supporting detail needed to satisfy the requirements. Then take the HLD and expand with details for accomplishing that phase.

The process is slightly different in Agile, with multiple parts within the design. Assume this diagram is the design for the entire solution, and the software has three main parts (the three large boxes). Each small box is considered a unit. The small units work together to generate output. Communication and information happen between the large boxes (integration). Sometimes you start with one large square as MVP and keep adding integration to expand the functionality.

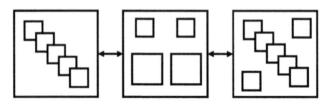

Figure 55 Main design

Once you reach this design level, each requirement should be a feature and a story. Each team takes one small box and starts building it. Ultimately, the teams test different parts to ensure the required output is functioning as required. Usually, the software is in pieces, as seen in the diagram. It used to be monolithic. Now everyone tries to reduce the units to achieve value quickly. So, it's best to divide the application into different parts.

Once one large box is completed, move to the next, and so on, until the software is complete. How you approach it is the key distinction between different development methods. For example, if you do the requirements and the design in one shot, then move to code, then deliver the final product to the customer, this is Waterfall. But if you validate with the customer at each step, this is the V model. Or you can approach the work incrementally by doing requirements in one shot but carrying out the design, coding, and testing in phases. Finally, you have a spiral model where you go through all the stages in small steps.

Agile, by contrast, is not a methodology per se. It's more of a mindset, that of being flexible with change. Scrum, XP, kanban, and the like were born from that. Any methodology that incorporates Agile focuses on building increments of product or knowledge gathering and continuously integrating small units into a product or service. In other words, you don't have to wait for the entire big box to be finished. You can finish the small box, launch the application, and keep adding units and testing integration.

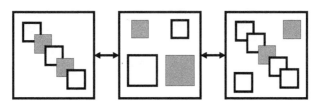

Figure 56 Design with developed features

For example, in Figure 56, it's possible to build the small dark boxes first because these add the most value to the software. Then you can continue to work on the other boxes based on their priority.

Typically (even in Agile), the overall design will not change; but small units in the design might be added, removed, or rearranged. This should not be a problem since the team builds units and continuously integrates them into the main software. This is why concepts like CI/CD are attractive to software industries—because they speed up the cycle time and move quickly from "what if" to the "actual deployment."

Phase Four: Release Planning

Release planning in Agile is multilevel, less up-front, but frequent. It includes:

- Daily planning, tasks, and story points
- Iteration planning (sprints)
- Release planning (single or multi-sprint)

It may sound intimidating, but it's more straightforward than that. Figure 57 summarizes how the final results should look.

You have the first column of your product broken into epics. Then these epics are broken down into stories. These stories are broken down further into story points (user statements). Each point is linked to a specific release and sprint. And all of this is linked to a group of tasks. Tasks usually are linked to each other in the project plan.

Note: Sometimes, story points are numerical to show the effort required in this point.

Product	Epics	Stories	Story points	Release	Sprints	Tasks
Important product	Epic 1	Story 1	S1 P1	R1	S1	T1–T5
			S1 P2	R1	S1	T6–T7
		Story 2	S2 P1	R1	S1	T8–T10
			S2 P2	R2	S2	T11
	Epic 2	Story 3	S3 P1	R2	S3	T12, T15–T22
			S3 P2	R2	S3	T35–T40
			S3 P3	R3	S4	T41–T48
		Story 4	S4 P1	R3	S5	T45–T50
			S4 P2	R4	S6	T51–T60

Figure 57 Release planning

How to decide on the release? There are three ways:

- **Value-driven**—based on the requirements of specific features patched together to deliver value to the business
- **Time driven**—every X number of sprints (based on the velocity)
- **Fixed schedule**—every two weeks or every month on a specific date, whatever is ready will be released

Deciding on which way the versions are released is usually the project manager's responsibility. There are two ways to track these releases—release burnup and storyboard.

Release Burnup

The release burns up in two main lines, customer requirements (stories) and the features built. The project ends when the two lines meet.

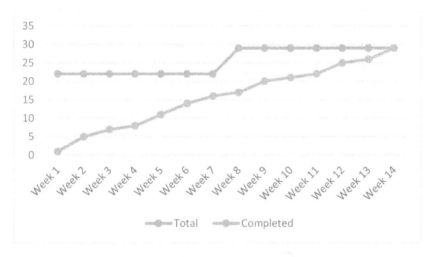

Figure 58 Release burnup

In Figure 58, please take note of week7. The client added some additional stories, which led to more requirements, which, in turn, increased the number of features. The reverse occurs if the customer removes features. This chart demonstrates the overall project progress.

The Task Board

This is the same concept as the kanban board (chapter 5). The board (usually a physical board) tracks each step's progress and, when done, indicates the next step. This is a very useful way to track sprint progress.

Backlog	Analysis		Development		Testing	Released	Deployed
	Ongoing	Done	Ongoing	Done			
Task A	X						
Task B		X					
Task C				X			
Task D						X	
Task E					X		

Figure 59 Task board

Phase Five: Delivery, Build, Learn, and Improve

In the delivery phase, aside from building the code (the process is covered in another book), three main activities are needed

- Daily Scrum (daily stand-up, daily huddle)
- Backlog cleanup
- Retrospectives

Daily Scrum (Daily Stand-Up, Daily Huddle)

At the start of each day, in the form of a short, participant-driven sync stand-up, often lasting no more than 15 minutes, each person shares progress and describes any obstacles, usually while in front of the task board. This session aims to answer just three questions:

- What did you accomplish yesterday?
- What will you do today?
- Can you outline any blockers in your way?

You will encounter two challenges in the daily stand-up:

- People will hold back and not speak.
- People will not show up.

Resolutions to the challenges:

- Consider passing around a speaking token. Whoever receives it speaks to the rest of the group and is obliged to answer the three questions cited.
- If people are not showing up for the daily stand-up, there are options:

- Make the rounds 15 minutes before the meeting and personally ask for attendance. Send a reminder by email.
- Ask top management to attend from time to time.
- Serve snacks and donuts. (Breakfast, in general, is very effective.)

Note: Such daily stand-up is not called a *meeting* to avoid forming a meeting agenda and having a formal structure. It's a fast-paced chat. If the team needs to sit down, it turns into a progress review meeting, which is strongly not recommended in an Agile setup.

Backlog Cleanup

The project's duration remains at least the same as with Waterfall (usually longer). Though the project is Agile, project duration will still be measured in months or years, similar to Waterfall. The difference is Agile's ability to adapt to change. Part of the change means that there is a need to conduct a backlog cleanup, which includes:

- Removing user stories that are no longer relevant
- Creating new user stories
- Changing the priorities of the stories
- Correcting estimates
- Splitting or merging user stories

Retrospectives

Retrospectives are useful in creating the development review. The review reflects the body of completed work and brings valuable information to all stakeholders about what went well and what went wrong. There are two approaches to the retrospectives:

- **Per sprint**: The focus is on the sprint, usually with the team, and it contains technical information.
- **Per project**: The focus is on the project and includes all sprints, usually with the stakeholders, and usually is focused on the business information (budget, timeline, and so on).

Phase Six: UAT and Training

In this phase, two main activities happen:

- User acceptance testing (usually happens as a sprint review meeting)
- Training (informal training on the newly created function)

Sprint Review Meeting

A meeting is held at the end of the sprint to demonstrate the product developed in the sprint. The Scrum master holds the meeting and helps to keep it on track. People share their feedback openly. Here is an example of the agenda:

1. Recap sprint goal.
2. Conduct a product demonstration (as realistic as possible from whatever is designated as "done").
3. The product owner approves a completed feature from the backlog.
4. Collect feedback from stakeholders.

The team also needs to conduct a user study to ensure the product is usable. If the user doesn't like the product or finds it hard to use, consider their comments in upcoming sprints since no product is valuable if no one uses it. During ease-of-use testing, users must give feedback or be observed by experts. Users should be directed to achieve a specific goal (a function typically performed in daily life). This is not a product acceptance test. This is merely to collect feedback to make the product more user-friendly.

Here are a few terminologies helpful for this phase:

- **Software walkthrough**: Opening the code and walking through every part of it and how it should function to highlight any potential issue.
- **Software technical review**: Code improvement, overall design review, enhancement requirements.
- **Software inspections (QA)**: The testing phase.
- **Measurement**: A standard unit of measure, like cm or inch.
- **Metric**: Two or more measures to yield meaningful results, such as miles versus hours (distance versus time in this example).

- **Indicators**: Metrics are arranged into subgroups to emphasize one or more measurements.

Phase Seven: Deploy to Production

This is the final part of the sprint or the project. Currently, the operations team is usually being trained on the software features in preparation for receiving the handoff. In this phase, there are some things you need to consider from the operations side.

If the DevOps practice is still to be built or you don't have a CI/CD pipeline, the primary objective is to have a release package with service components compatible with one another. Your first decision is how to deploy it.

Select Deployment Phases

Three options are available:

- **Deployment in batches**: Each phase is composed of 20 percent of the total number of servers or workstations (or specific locations/sites)
- **Big Bang**: One phase, 100 percent
- **Pilot Big Bang**: Deployment in two phases:
  - **Phase one**: Collect feedback from a small group representative of the organization (selected users or servers), and deploy 5 percent first. During this pilot phase, collect feedback. Falling back from this position is easy since the impact will be limited. Usually, we select a diverse stakeholder group for this phase. Do not choose friendly, cooperative users. You need workaholics to test the system thoroughly.
  - **Phase two**: Adjust the plans with findings from phase one and deploy the remaining 95 percent.

Deployment Automation versus Manual Deployment

If possible, create a fully automated package, which will be much better than a manual deployment. Unfortunately, automation doesn't cover all cases. In some cases, automation will take much longer. You must choose the approach. If the tasks are repeatable many times and are relatively straightforward with no logic or what-if scenarios, go with automation. Manual deployment will be quicker if you have a limited number of deployments.

Release Team Responsibilities

The release team's responsibility is to confirm that all service requirements are completed before the production release. The release plan should define the scope and contents of the release, risk assessment, stakeholders, and who is responsible for the release. After gathering the required information, create a checklist for each package. Here's an example:

- Is there enough capacity?
- Does the operation team have the capability to operate this service?
- Are documents signed off?
- Are software licenses, and so on, in place?

At the end of release management, create a lessons-learned document for future improvements.

Bonus Chapter: Agile Philosophy

Agile is not one method; Agile is both a philosophy and an umbrella term for a collection of methods or approaches that share common characteristics. You may understand the philosophy and then learn how to perform the overall method, though the methods employed increase by the day. So, knowing a general idea (the *why*) will make applying the method not as challenging.

Almost everyone knows that complexity is not desirable, but the question remains why this is the case. When building a new system, you create either a big, complex system or something simple. This chapter teaches you how to make a stable, complex system. Understanding complexity will enable you to deal with things you don't understand (*yet*) without holding these choices back until you do, which is usually the case when creating new software. You will also understand why the need for Agility is required.

What Is Complex?

A complex system is a system that requires constant adjustment to maintain its existence. This definition can be applied to many things:

- An ERP system inside an organization
- An organization inside a market
- A single market inside a country

The critical distinction between complex and noncomplex is that a complex system requires the maintenance of its existence. It needs to evolve and move continually.

The best way to understand a business problem is to have a bird's-eye view of it, to know how this problem integrates into the other areas and how it interacts with the other components of the complex system. In other words, how the software interacts in an organization you don't have full control over.

This high-level understanding is important in software development systems because software systems are systems, after all, and to build a good, stable system, the same rules apply, so it's good to know how complex systems work.

Types of Complex Systems

There are five levels of complex systems:

Type 1. Simple System

These are static systems, don't require changes, and don't evolve. This is a river, or a pile of rocks. Prediction of how these things will act in the future is simple.

Type 2. "Simple Complex" Systems

All components are well-behaved and obey predictable rules. Usually, things start out this way before becoming infinitely complex. Prediction of these systems is difficult. Still, it's possible with a high level of certainty with things like the simulation of patterns of moving objects or the movement of planets and asteroids, for example. It's difficult, but with enough computing power, you can model it.

Type 3. "Infinitely Complex" Systems

These are the bigger systems with multiple simple complex systems inside, linked together so that one system affects all other systems, which causes an endless chain reaction.

This means that systems A impact B, B impact A, and so on, in an infinite loop. This is the simplest form of infinitely complex systems, but on a larger scale, they could contain hundreds of "simple complex" systems, each impacting the others in an infinite loop.

Sometimes the impact going back and forth will generate some random variation, which means that the system, due to variation, changes unexpectedly. In other words, the more "simple complex" systems you have, the more the possibility for variation will exist.

The way this "infinitely complex" system deals with these variations is by creating new, small "simple complex" systems, and these systems become part of the "infinitely complex" system. And, in turn, the variations increase, and new systems are created. This is why it's called the "infinitely complex"—because it will continue creating systems to address the variation.

For example, you need an email system for the users. This system's components are users and the email system, which creates a "simple complex" system. Both users and the email system will impact each other, but you cannot predict when the users will use the system.

Adding supporting systems: This email system will require authentication to hold user's passwords, and a need for file sharing is required to share large files. These new systems are components of the whole system, but they are still simple.

Adding connections to other systems: You need to be able to send things (data, email) outside of the organization. You will need to secure this system. The internet is an infinitely complex system, and it will continue to grow. And no one can predict what will happen with the internet as a whole.

Let's look at another example. The ERP system is a "simple complex" system, but the entire "information technology" system is an "infinitely complex" system. And these systems keep unpredictably impacting each other. This is why most IT systems need constant maintenance to stay operational. Otherwise, if left unchecked, they will go down in a few days or weeks at most.

Now, the process mentioned in the infinitely complex system sometimes doesn't go all the way to infinity. It may stop after specific changes and become stable. In this case, it becomes a sub–infinitely complex system or could turn into a large "simple complex" system. For example, cloud providers have these systems, but they limit what you can and cannot do. Everything follows a very strict automation script, and their data centers become sub-infinitely complex. They still need tweaks but have way too many redundancies to fail. Though they fail from time to time, they manage to make the cycle length longer.

Type 4. "Complex Adaptive" Systems

These are unpredictable systems. The parts in these systems are both "simple complex" and "infinitely complex" systems. Each piece is trying to reach a specific goal while maintaining its impact on other parts of the system.

The system's changes are generated from the pieces themselves, not the pieces' interactions, because each one is pushing to reach its objective. In this case, the role of the interactions is to either speed up the change, slow it down, or even reorganize the entire system. For example, you have many companies in the information technology industry, each fulfilling a specific function for the IT customer. This is called the *IT market*. Each of these companies has its objective (to build, sell, grow, and so on). Some compete, and some complement each other.

But if you pay attention, you will discover that the interactions speed up the change from time to time. Like how the COVID-19 lockdowns sped up video conferencing application development, or how one company acquired and merged with another company, changing the whole system. These interactions changed the whole market (the same as when Dell acquired EMC or when IBM acquired Red Hat). These significant interactions led to changes in the dynamics.

Type 5. Ecosystem and Living Systems

These are huge systems containing multiple types of systems—including simple, "simple complex," infinitely complex, and "adaptive complex" systems—that achieve a balance (this could be a company, an entire country, or even the total global market).

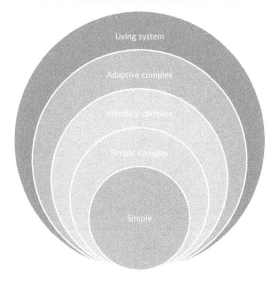

Figure 60 System complexity

All of these five layers comprise a static view. You could take this snapshot and try to predict where it will go next.

Now let's add the passing of time to these systems to understand better how they will behave.

Adding Time

Next, we add the passage of time to an ecosystem, for example, the accumulation of information. The decision-making in such a system becomes more difficult over time until no decision can be made. Then the entire system collapses, and the process starts over once more.

In other words, the more complex the system, the less is the chance of its survival, or it has to be smart to prevail.

(Smart = Agility + Adaptiveness)

This is why Agile is booming. Without it, the system will collapse (as mentioned, the system could be a whole company). You have to be agile to address the variations happening in the bigger system. The faster you handle them, the less impact these variations will have on your complex system stability.

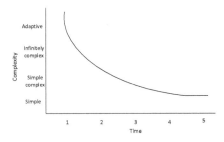

Figure 61 Time and complexity

In Figure 61, the time unit varies from 1 to 5. It could be months, years, decades, or more. You determine the time unit based on the system level you are measuring. In other words:

- Companies are measured in 10-year units.
- In the case of a market, 1 unit = 50 years.
- For whole countries, 1 unit = 100 to 1000 years.

It's the nature of things to get less complex, to start over building more complexity, and succeeding in each round to sustain complexity for a longer and longer duration of time.

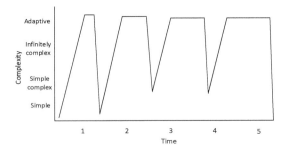

Figure 62 Sustaining system complexity

Usually, system failure is due to unforeseen feedback effects. The data built up inside the system generates more variations that the system is not smart enough to address. (This is why many IT problems go away when you simply restart the system.)

One of the common complex systems is enterprise-wide systems. In such a system, the components are known, but the interactions are not known. Such systems require constant change and adjustment over time.

ERP is a "simple complex" example with great complexity, but still you can predict its behavior and even control it to a certain degree. Agility aims at a higher standard. The business is part of the market, so whatever the business changes, no matter how small, will change the overall system status. You will then have two choices: to continue if the outcome is desirable, or pivot if the outcome is less desirable. In the latter case, a quick reaction to the market could mean the organization's survival.

Throughout this book, you may have noticed a pattern. Most technologies are created to respond to complex system variations or even control system interactions to reduce unexpected variations to very low levels.

www.ingramcontent.com/pod-product-compliance
Lightning Source LLC
LaVergne TN
LVHW051247050326
832903LV00028B/2613